C000129597

A BOOK OF SAINTS AND HEROES

A BOOK OF SAINTS AND HEROES

JOANNA BOGLE

GRACEWING

First published in England in 2013
by
Gracewing
2 Southern Avenue
Leominster
Herefordshire HR6 0QF
United Kingdom
www.gracewing.co.uk

No part of this publication may be reproduced, stored in a
retrieval system, or transmitted in any form or by any means,
electronic, mechanical, photocopying, recording or otherwise,
without the written permission of the publisher.

The right of Joanna Bogle to be identified
as the author of this work has been asserted in accordance
with the Copyright, Designs and Patents Act 1988.

© 2013 Joanna Bogle

ISBN 978 085244 809 0

Typeset by Gracewing

Cover design by Bernardita Peña Hurtado

CONTENTS

Contents...v

Introduction...vii

1 St Peter, the first Pope..1

2 St Andrew, patron of Scotland....................................7

3 St George, patron of England.....................................11

4 St David of Wales...15

5 St Patrick, patron of Ireland..19

6 St Augustine, missionary to Kent................................23

7 St Thomas Becket, martyr of Canterbury...................29

8 St Thomas More, Chancellor of England....................33

9 St Edmund Campion, tortured but unbroken..............37

10 St Damien of Molokai, hero of the forgotten.............43

11 Blessed John Henry Newman, leading people to the Light.....49

12 St Charles Lwanga and his companions, heroes of Africa.....53

13 Father Willie Doyle, hero of the trenches...................59

14 Blessed Rupert Mayer, soldier and saint...................65

15 Emperor Karl, soldier and peacemaker.....................71

16 Father John Hawes, the builder in the bush..............75

17 The Mexican Martyrs: "Viva Cristo Rey!"........................79

18 St Maximilian Kolbe, martyr for charity........................85

19 Bishop Count von Galen, the "lion of Munster"..............91

20 Blessed Marcel Callo, patron of youth...........................97

21 Cardinal Josef Slipyj, witness to the Gulag...............101

22 Father Jerzy, hero of Poland...107

23 Father Christian de Chergé and the Atlas monks.......115

24 Father Pino, Martyred by the Mafia...........................121

25 The great John Paul..125

INTRODUCTION

Be open to his voice resounding in the depths of your heart: even now his heart is speaking to your heart. Christ has need of families to remind the world of the dignity and beauty of family life. He needs men and women to devote their lives to the noble task of education, tending the young and forming them in the ways of the Gospel. He needs those who will consecrate their lives to the service of perfect charity, following him in chastity, poverty and obedience and serving him in the least of our brothers and sisters. He needs the powerful love of the contemplative religious, who sustain the Church's witness and activity through their constant prayer. And he needs priests, good and holy priests, men who are willing to lay down their lives for their sheep. Ask Our Lord what he has in mind for you! Ask him for the generosity to say "Yes!" Do not be afraid to give yourself totally to Jesus.

Pope Benedict XVI, *Speech to young people in London, 2010.*

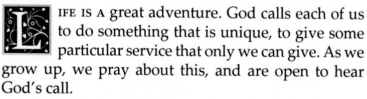 IFE IS A great adventure. God calls each of us to do something that is unique, to give some particular service that only we can give. As we grow up, we pray about this, and are open to hear God's call.

This book is about men who did that. They are heroes, men who put a priority on God and on truth, on serving others and on doing the right thing. They knew that these things are much more important than personal comfort or well-being.

Reading the stories of heroes can be exciting, but also a bit daunting. It can make us think "Would I be brave enough to do that?" But people aren't born brave. They acquire courage as we can acquire other virtues—by prayer and by practice.

Today there are still martyrs for the Faith—and people who endure hardship and difficulty rather than betray what they know to be true.

In this book, I have written about some of the great saints and heroes from long ago—St Peter, the very first Pope, St Thomas More, who lived and died under King Henry VIII. But half of the book is about men who lived in more modern times—including the twentieth century and one who lived into the twenty-first. These are men whose lives really are quite close to our own. And who will be the saints and heroes of the years to come?

Joanna Bogle
15 August 2013, Solemnity of the Assumption

1

SAINT PETER
THE FIRST POPE

FISHERMAN, A HARD-WORKING man who owned his own small fishing co-operative along with his brother Andrew. A married man—probably a widower by the time we meet him. Peter was called by Jesus Christ, and left everything and followed him.

Peter is mentioned more times—far many more times—than any other Apostle in the Gospels. It is he who is called specifically by Christ to be a "fisher of men". He has his name changed by Christ—just as God changed Abram's name to Abraham in the Old Testament. "Abram" means "father" and "Abraham" means "father of many". Peter's original name was Simon, but Christ gave him a new name, Peter, the "rock". He will be the rock on which the Church is founded. And Christ gave him "the keys to the kingdom of Heaven". This echoes an important passage in the Old Testament, where God calls a man named Eliakim and gives him authority: "And he shall be like a father to the inhabitants of Jerusalem and to the house of Judah. And I will place the key of the house of David upon his shoulder. And when he opens, no one will close. And when he closes, no one will open" (Is. 22: 20–24).

Thus Jesus made Peter the first Pope. The other Apostles would recognise him as their leader, and with him they would one day start the process that would take the Gospel of Jesus Christ all over the world, and down through all the ages. You are reading this book today and understanding it, because Peter and the others did as Christ asked.

Peter needed courage to be a follower of Christ. At first, he must have been very puzzled, not understanding who Jesus really was. But as a devout Jew, he was looking forward to the coming of the Messiah. He would have thought about it and prayed about it, and talked about it with his brother Andrew. The day that Jesus gave him the "keys to the kingdom of Heaven" was an important one. Jesus and the disciples were on a journey up to Jerusalem. When they reached Caesaria Philippi—a significant place, marking the halfway point on their journey—Jesus asked "Who do people say the Son of Man is?" He wanted them to tell him who they thought he was. They told him that some people thought he was John the Baptist, or Elijah or one of the prophets. There was a belief that Elijah, one of the greatest of the prophets of long ago, would one day return. Jesus pressed them:"But who do you say that I am" and it was Peter who replied:"You are the Christ, the Son of the Living God" (Matthew 16:15–16). He had understood. It was his statement of faith. And so Jesus was able to give him the authority to be the "rock" on which the Church would be established.

When Jesus was arrested, and taken away to be tortured and crucified, Peter was not brave. As he was warming himself in the courtyard of the high priest's house, a maid came up and said "You were also with Jesus the Gallilean!" but he denied it. He did this three times. And then a cock crew and he remembered that Jesus had once told him "Before the cock crows, you will have denied me three times". He went out and wept bitterly.

Now the only reason we know about this is because Peter himself told about it. He could have kept the story to himself But he was honest: he wanted us to know the truth. And he was courageous too—later on, he would give up his own life rather than deny Jesus again. And down all the years since then, Christians across the world have been able to face up to their own failures and sins and mistakes, and find new hope in the forgiveness of God and in the example of St Peter.

After the death and resurrection of Christ, Peter was acknowledged by everyone as the leader of the little band of followers who were the beginnings of the Church on earth. It was Mary Magdalene who first saw the risen Christ in the garden on that Easter Sunday morning. She at first thought he was the gardener! But then he spoke to her and she knew his voice, and greeted him with joy. She ran to tell Peter and the other Apostles the good news. They hurried to the tomb—and the others stood back to let Peter in first. He saw the empty tomb, and he believed.

Christ told the Apostles to take the Gospel everywhere: "Go therefore and make disciples of all nations, baptising them in the name of the Father and the Son and the Holy Spirit, teaching them to observe all that I have commanded you, and lo, I am with you always, to the end of the age" (Matthew 28:19–10).

Peter knew that the capital city of the world at that time was Rome. He would have thought and prayed long and hard about this. Surely he should go to Rome, to take the Gospel there? All the evidence is that he did so—and established the Church in Rome, where it has had a base ever since. After he died, a new

Pope—the word means "father"—was chosen, and there has been an unbroken line of Popes ever since.

When St Peter arrived in Rome he was just a fisherman who had been given an enormous task. When he was a boy, he could not have imagined that this huge adventure lay before him. Now, as a man, he had to puzzle it out. We can imagine him walking by the Tiber river. Perhaps for a moment he thought of the fish swimming in it and thought about the days when he was a busy fisherman with his own boat. But now he had to be a "fisher of men". He had a commission from Jesus Christ, the Son of the Living God.

The early Church in Rome was persecuted by the pagan Roman authorities. They did not want this new religion. Peter was arrested, but was released from prison by a miracle—an angel came to him in the night and let him out. He was able to continue his work of spreading the Gospel and building up the Church. But later he was arrested again and this time he was led out to a hill beyond the city—the Vatican Hill—to be executed. He was to be crucified. He said that he was not worthy to die in the same way as his Master, Jesus Christ, had done and so at his request he was crucified upside-down. The place where he suffered and died is now where St Peter's Square stands. His body was buried on the hill and now today a great basilica is dedicated to him

Peter—man of prayer, man of courage. Peter, the man on whom rested the huge responsibility of taking on the leadership of the group of Apostles who would start to spread the Gospel through the world. Today, you can still visit the places where he fished along the shores of Galilee. And you can visit the great basilica which bears his name in Rome. And Peter himself is in Heaven, close to Christ whom he loved and served while they were both on earth.

2

St Andrew, patron of Scotland

HE NAME ANDREW means "manly" or "brave". Andrew was a fisherman, born at Bethsaida by the Sea of Galilee. He was the brother of Simon—later to be called Peter—and they ran a family fishing business together.

When John the Baptist began to preach about repentance, Andrew went to hear him. He was inspired to become one of his followers. But John the Baptist was really pointing to someone greater: Jesus Christ. When Jesus walked by, John called out "Behold the Lamb of God!" Andrew and another Apostle followed Jesus, who asked them "What do you seek?". Andrew said "Where do you live?" and Jesus said "Come and see". They went with him and spent the next hours with him. Andrew was convinced: this was the Messiah, the one promised by God to Israel. He went to his brother Simon and told him "We have found the Messiah".

This was the beginning of the great adventure of St Andrew's life. He and his brother Simon-Peter left their fishing boats and nets and all that they had known to follow Christ. Through them and the other Apostles, the Gospel of Jesus Christ would be spread through the whole world.

We can follow something of St Andrew's life in the New Testament. The Gospel of St John describes the Feeding of the Five Thousand. A great crowd of people had started to follow Jesus, and they were hungry. It was drawing near to the time of the Passover, the great feast of the Jews that marked their liberation from slavery. This coming Passover, although no one except Christ knew it, would have a greater and deeper importance than any that had gone before—an eternal significance for the whole human race. As the great crowd gathered, Jesus asked how it would be possible to give them something to eat—although he already knew the answer. Andrew spoke up, pointing out a boy who had five loaves and two fishes "but what are they among so many?" And Jesus told him to make the people sit down, and he took the loaves, and gave thanks, and distributed them, and the same with the fish ... and everyone had plenty to eat, and afterwards twelve baskets were filled with the fragments of bread that was left over. Later Jesus spoke to them about himself as the Bread of Life:"I am the bread of life; he who comes to me shall not hunger, and he who believes in me shall never thirst..." The people knew that long years before God had provided manna in the desert. Now here was Jesus Christ speaking about himself as bread, as "living bread which came down from heaven".

After Christ's death and Resurrection and Ascension into Heaven, and after the great drama of Pentecost, the Apostles went out to preach the Gospel and travelled far, far away from the lands they had always known. We do not know the details of St Andrew's travels, but one account claims that he went as far as the Black Sea and headed out to what is now Ukraine and Russia, getting as far as the cities of Kiev and Novgorod. Certainly there has been an unbroken devotion to him in those territories for hundreds and hundreds of years.

Like his brother St Peter, Andrew met his death through martyrdom. The pagans were challenged by the new message of Christ. The old pagan gods did not make such demands. They could not understand why the Christians could not simply recognise Christ as one among many gods. They were angry that something so great and world-changing was happening. They wanted to keep it away.

Tradition says that St Andrew was martyred at Patras in Greece, and that he was crucified on an X-shaped cross. This form of cross is that always described as a "St Andrew's cross". There is now a church on the site, and great devotion to St Andrew there.

How did St Andrew come to be associated with Scotland? In the 7th century, some relics of St Andrew were brought to Scotland, and a great devotion to him began. The cross of St Andrew is Scotland's flag, and thus forms part of the Union Flag of the United Kingdom. Scotland's most ancient university is in the town of St Andrews. It is the oldest university in the English-speaking world. The town used to be the ecclesiastical capital of Scotland, but the great Cathedral there was destroyed at the Reformation—its ruins now stand starkly on the hills by the sea. St Andrew is also the patron saint of Ukraine, Russia, Romania, and towns in Italy, Malta and Portugal.

3

St George, patron of England

S t George has his feast day on 23 April. He is the patron saint of England. He lived in the 4th century—400 years after the birth of Christ, and his home was in the Middle East, in what is today Israel. It was then part of the Roman Empire, and the Emperor was named Diocletian. George held the rank of Tribune (roughly Colonel) in the Roman Army.

The Emperor Diocletian had at first been very friendly towards Christians. They were loyal, hard-working and good citizens. But then it became clear that they did not regard him as a god, and did not put his claims and those of the Empire before everything else. They worshipped one God, and had their first loyalty to him, and to him alone.

The Emperor put pressure on the Christians. He issued notices which were put up in public places. All Christians must affirm their full loyalty to him and to the Empire by offering sacrifices to the gods—and if they failed to do this they would have their homes seized and would eventually be arrested themselves.

George was personally known to the Emperor. He was a loyal Roman with a brave record of service. His father had also been a senior Army officer and public official. No one really wanted to arrest George. But he refused to renounce his Christian faith and so he was thrown into prison. Many people came to see him to persuade him out of his commitment to Christ. Eventually, persuasion gave way to threats and then to torture. He had been offered property, slaves and honours — these eventually gave way to vicious use of torture equipment. George had given away his property and all his wealth to the poor when he knew he was to be arrested, and declared his faith openly and repeatedly. He was finally executed on 23 April 303 — which was Good Friday. The place where he died was Lydda — today it is called Lodd, and it is still a town and rich in history. This part of the world is the Holy Land — where Christ himself lived.

Ancient documents hail George as one of the greatest of the martyrs of the fourth century. Very quickly, devotion to him spread across the empire. It reached Britain: there were churches here named in his honour.

When the Angles and Saxons invaded Britain, they became Christian in their turn (see the story about St Augustine) and they came to know about St George. But what really made him famous was many years later, when English soldiers went to the Middle East. They were fighting in wars there, trying to defend the holy places where Jesus himself lived and died. In the battles, they longed to have saints praying for them in Heaven. They learned about St George, and visited Lydda where he had died. They found that there were churches dedicated to him. They prayed to him and felt that he was protecting them.

When the English soldiers came home, they brought with them their Crusaders' Flag — a red cross on a white background. This became the flag of St George. Today it forms part of the Union Jack, the national flag of Britain.

Ever since that time, St George has been England's special patron. There are images of him in stained glass in many churches. Sometimes he is shown in war memorials, with his sword. A story says that he once killed a dragon to save a young girl—it's a reminder that he was a brave soldier who wanted to help the poor and defenceless.

When someone in Britain has done something very splendid he or she may be given the Order of the Garter. It is our highest Order of Chivalry. It is given at St George's Chapel at Windsor, the chapel attached to the Royal family's castle. The Queen gives the honour "in the name of God, Our Lady and St George."

There are churches in Britain named in honour of St George, and a chapel in London's Westminster Cathedral dedicated to him. In that chapel, soldiers who died in the two World Wars of the twentieth century are remembered—because St George was a soldier and so this is the right place to honour them.

4

ST DAVID OF WALES

T DAVID WAS a monk, who lived a tough, austere life and planted Christianity strongly and deeply in Wales and in Brittany and Cornwall. He lived and worked in the 6th century. At that time, while there was a strong Christianity which went back to Roman times among the Celtic people, much of the rest of Europe was still pagan. The pagan Angles and Saxons had invaded what was now being called England, and the Romano-British Celtic Christians had fled westwards.

David—Dewi in Welsh—is said to have been the illegitimate son of a king. He become a monk, and gained fame as a preacher and teacher. He gathered around him other men who wanted to dedicate their lives wholly to God and live simply in poverty, chastity, and obedience.

Their lives included no luxuries: they were known as "the watermen" because they did not drink any beer or other alcohol. They ploughed their own land, dragging the plough themselves instead of using horses. They grew wheat to make bread and ate it with herbs, never having any meat. All their possessions were held in common.

David's motto is still known in Wales: "Do the little things in life" —in Welsh: "Gwnewch y pethau bychain mewn bywyd". His influence was huge: people were attracted by his message about the love and mercy that

God wants to pour out on to all men, and they liked the fact that he lived this message with courage and simplicity, lacking pomp or any sense of self-importance. He went on pilgrimage to Jerusalem—a long and dangerous journey at that time, and he walked most of the way, begging for his simple needs as he went. In Jerusalem he was anointed as Bishop of Wales. He travelled back—again on foot—and took responsibility for taking the Gospel to all the Welsh people.

David established a monastery at the place that still bears his name—St David's in Pembrokeshire. He became a trusted leader, and people flocked to hear his preaching. A famous miracle is associated with him: on one occasion, when he was preaching at Brefi, people called out that they could not see or hear him—a mound is said to have risen up underneath him, so that he was standing on a hill in full view of everyone and his words carried. A white dove settled on his shoulder. The hill is still there and the place is called of Llanddewi Brefi in his honour. St David is often depicted with a white dove to commemorate this incident.

When St David died, his last words were "Be joyful, keep the Faith, and do the little things". Legend says that after he died, the monastery was filled with the sound of angels singing, as his soul was taken up to Paradise. He was buried in the cathedral at St David's and for many hundreds of years people visited his shrine there. His feast day is still celebrated in Wales—it is on 1 March.

St David is said to have visited the Abbey at Glastonbury in Somerset and to have been responsible for its extension so that it became one of the biggest abbeys in Britain. Based in Wales, he sent monks as missionaries to Cornwall, to Brittany and to parts of Ireland. To this day there is evidence of a Celtic Christianity with its distinctive elaborate crosses in all of these places.

In the Central Lobby of the Houses of Parliament in London, where people go to meet their Members of Parliament, there are big mosaic showing the four saints of the British Isles: St George, St Andrew, St Patrick and St David.

5

St Patrick, Patron of Ireland

I N THE FOURTH century, Britain had been part of the Roman Empire for three hundred years. Christianity had been brought at a very early date, and the Church was well established. But the Empire was crumbling, the Roman legions were departing to fight battles elsewhere, and pagan Saxons were invading from the East.

Patrick was a Romano-Briton, born in about the year 387 on the western coast in Britain, possible in Wales or possibly in Cumbria. He was a Christian and his father was a deacon. When he was about sixteen, he was captured from his home by pirates who had crossed the sea from Ireland on a raiding-party. They took Patrick as a slave back to Ireland where he worked on farms. Finally, when he was in his early twenties, he was able to escape and he managed to get aboard a ship and return home.

His years of captivity and exile had brought him closer to God and had confirmed an already strong conviction that he was meant to be a priest. We do not know where he studied or was ordained—it seems possible that it was at Glastonbury, the great monastic centre in the West (in what is now Somerset). Here, legend says, Joseph of Arimithea visited from the Holy Land, bringing a precious relic, the Chalice from the

Last Supper, and planting his staff in the ground where it grew into the famous Glastonbury Thorn. Certainly Glastonbury was a flourishing centre of Romano-British Christianity and regarded as a place of great holiness and spiritual significance.

Patrick obtained permission to return to Ireland as a missionary bishop: he wanted to establish among the pagan people there a knowledge and love of Christ.

He faced enormous hardships—the people were bound by laws and customs and traditions that made it complicated for any stranger to make his message understood, and the pagan beliefs were deep-rooted. But he persevered. Patrick preached in the north and west of Ireland, eventually establishing a strong Church in the whole island, which has remained to this day.

There had been a legend among the pagans that one day a man would come from across the sea bringing a new message. He would wear a strange hat with a hole in it—(perhaps that is Patrick's mitre?)—and carry a stick curled over at the top (his crozier?). The legend spoke of how he would teach people things that they would later all recite together.

Patrick is the patron saint of Ireland and there are many places associated with him. These include Saul in County Down, where it is said he opened his first church in a farm-building given to him by a local chieftain called Dichu, and the Hill of Slane where he is said to have taught about the Holy Trinity using the little three-leaved shamrock plant that grows everywhere. To this day, people walk up Croagh Patrick, the mountain named after him: there is a traditional pilgrimage there each July. And, above all, people go to Lough Derg in County Donegal to make a tough and difficult three day retreat of fasting and prayer, with nothing to eat or drink except black tea.

Patrick preached to the tribal leaders and kings, and to their families. When the leaders were won over to the Faith, the people had to follow. He established monasteries and convents—often ladies from rich and powerful families chose to accept the full challenge of their new-found Christian faith and take vows of poverty to live in a convent. Stories and legends were passed around about him: he was said to be able to conjure up fire from Heaven, and that he challenged the druid religious leaders to prove their own powers and they revealed that they had none.

His teachings were tough—he emphasised penance and renouncing sin. The beautiful rugged landscape and the cold wet weather of autumn, winter and spring, the strong winds from the sea along all the coasts, have become identified with his strong and challenging message. Over the next centuries, missionaries would go out from Ireland to every corner of the world— China, India, Africa, the Americas—as missionaries, and would take with them the stories of St Patrick that they had learned from their parents and grandparents, who in turn had learned it from earlier generations.

One of the most famous stories associated with St Patrick is that he banished all the snakes from Ireland, and it is certainly a fact that it is one place in Europe where no snakes can be found to this day.

Patrick has been honoured in Ireland down all the centuries. His feast day is 17 March, which is a public holiday. Irish people who have emigrated to other countries—notably America and Australia—have built churches and cathedrals named in his honour and celebrate St Patrick's Day on a huge scale. Patrick himself is said to have been buried at what is today called Downpatrick in County Down.

6

ST AUGUSTINE, MISSIONARY TO KENT

HERE ARE TWO great saints called Augustine in the Church, and both are worth learning about. One is Saint Augustine of Hippo. He was a Bishop at a very important time, just as the Roman Empire was crumbling and no one quite knew what was to take its place. He gave people strong and clear teaching, and his writings have come down to us, showing the unchanging and glorious truths of the Christian faith that still make sense to us today. We know that at a time of change we can trust God and the Church and live by what is true and beautiful, and we need not be afraid.

The other Augustine is Saint Augustine of Canterbury. It is important for people in the English-speaking world to know about him. He wasn't a hero to begin with—on his first missionary journey to Britain he turned back. But then, in obedience to the Pope he set out again, and this time something lasting was achieved. Here is the story.

The Christian Faith came to Britain in the days of the Roman Empire—that same Roman Empire into which Jesus Christ was born in Bethlehem. The Roman Empire was vast and strong. After Jesus died and rose again, and ascended into Heaven, the Apostles took the Faith everywhere they could. Over the years the

Christian message spread. We do not know when it first reached Britain, but it was at a very early date, and when we find old Roman remains here we find Christian symbols and evidence that they were living as Christians, with Mass being celebrated and the Christian message taught.

But as the Roman Empire crumbled, people began invading from mainland Europe—Saxons and Angles from what is today Saxony and other parts of Germany. They arrived along the eastern coasts and settled in Britain. The original British were pushed westwards. The Saxons called them the "Welsh" or "strangers" and towns like Wallington in Surrey and Wallingford in Berkshire get their names from this, as of course does the country of Wales—these were places where the British lived.

The new Saxon arrivals were pagans. They had many different gods, and we still name some of the days of the week after them: Mars the god of war (Monday) Tiu, the god of duty (Tuesday), Woden (Wednesday) Thor, the god of thunder (Thursday) Freia the goddess (Friday).

The Angles and Saxons established themselves and today there are place-names which echo this: the country is called England (Angle-land) and there are places like Sussex (south Saxons) and Essex (east Saxons). There were wars and battles with the Britons. By the sixth century, there were a number of Saxon kingdoms. The king of one southern kingdom was Ethelbert, and he was married to Bertha, a princess from Gaul (France). She was a Christian, and she longed for her husband to be one, too. She sent word to the Pope in Rome and begged him to send some missionaries.

The Pope, Gregory the Great, knew about England. There were Anglo- Saxon slaves in Rome: one day he saw some in the Trajan Market and asked about them. He was told "They are Angles, from Angle-land", and he is said to have replied that they must be sent missionaries so as to become Christians and thus "Non Angli, sed Angeli" ("not Angles, but angels"). He summoned a group of Benedictine monks and asked them to undertake this task.

The monks, led by Augustine, were afraid. It was a long journey to England, and as they left Italy and travelled across France they heard more and more about the pagan people they would encounter once they set foot on English soil. They learned that these people were cruel and crude, that they worshipped many gods and knew nothing of Christian truth and Christian charity. The land was cold and grim and there had been many wars there, with the Saxons establishing themselves only after bitter fighting. Augustine and his monks turned back and went home to Rome.

The Pope was disappointed. He was also firm: they must retrace their steps, and go to England. Their mission must be accomplished. There was no retreat from this. They set off again. Augustine urged his monks onward. This time they must not fail.

On the orders of King Ethelbert, on the coast of Kent there were people looking out every day across the sea for ships that might be bringing messengers from Rome. Augustine and his monks were expected. No one knew when they would come—but letters had been received announcing that they were on their way. When they arrived, the king was ready to receive them.

Conversion to Christianity does not happen all at once. And when it does come, it may occur for a number of reasons. Ethelbert knew that somehow the old pagan gods did not really make sense any more — he wanted to be a real king of a viable kingdom, not just the leader of a rural settlement, based on survival and war. He wanted contacts with the wider world, he wanted a community that included men of knowledge. Presumably his wife had spoken of the glories of Christian civilisation, of the significance of distant Rome and how Christianity had supplanted the ancient pagan ways and was achieving a new sense of unity and purpose. Could the Saxons, on this island, remain bleakly aloof from all that was wise and interesting and useful?

In due course, Ethelbert was baptised and his whole kingdom became Christian. Augustine and his monks made contact with the British Christians whose traditions went back to Roman times. The next years would bring tensions between these "British" Christians, sometimes called "Celtic" Christians, and the new English ones. Augustine brought news and information from Rome: to some of the British Christians he may have seemed an upstart, a newcomer brandishing his Roman credentials. It would take some while before unity was achieved.

Today, a cross marks the place near Ramsgate in Kent where St Augustine landed, and the great Cathedral at Canterbury stands where he built his first church. There is a church dedicated to St Ethelbert in Ramsgate, and a great Abbey that bears St Augustine's name. There are Benedictine nuns at Minster, living in an abbey that dates back to Saxon times. In London's Westminster Cathedral there is a mosaic showing Pope

St Gregory the Great talking to the Anglo-Saxon slave boys in Rome. The name Augustine, or its shorter form, Austin, is still given to boys at baptism. And the faith that St Augustine planted still survives in England.

7

ST THOMAS BECKET, MARTYR OF CANTERBURY

ONG AGO, CAROL singing and collecting alms for the poor at Christmas time was known as "going a-Thomassing". This was in honour of St Thomas Becket, whose feast-day falls on 29 December, during the Christmas season.

St Thomas Becket is one of the best-known saints in England and people still flock to Canterbury and learn his story. He was appointed Archbishop of Canterbury in 1162 and died on 29 December 1170 in the cathedral at Canterbury at the hands of four assassins. His story is all bound up with the question of the freedom of the Church. It has a strong message for today.

Becket was born in London—in Cheapside, which is near St Paul's Cathedral. He was educated by monks at Merton Abbey, in what was then a rural area but is now part of South London, just outside Wimbledon and adjoining Tooting. The Abbey was destroyed along with all Britain's great religious houses under King Henry VIII, but there are still some fragments and remains. Today you can still visit Merton Abbey Mills and the park: the nearest tube station is known as Colliers Wood but also bears the words "Merton Abbey".

Becket was a gifted and intelligent man. While still young he obtained a position in the household of Theobald of Bec who became Archbishop of Canterbury. He studied canon law, and later carried out a number of important diplomatic tasks for the Archbishop. In due course his career prospered and the King, Henry II, appointed him Chancellor of the kingdom. He was not at that time a priest. He only became one when the king sought to nominate him as Archbishop of Canterbury. At that point, things changed in his life. He had been something of a careerist. But now he took stock and began to take his commitment to the Faith much more seriously. He fasted and said his Office faithfully, and he took his duties as Archbishop very seriously.

In particular, he opposed plans of the king—the Constitutions of Clarendon—which would have loosened the bond with Rome and given greater powers to the Crown and government in the life of the Church. At first, the differences between the King and the Archbishop did not seem very great. They had long been friends, and Henry had sent his son to Thomas for education in his household, much as Thomas himself had been sent to Theobald of Bec. The boy came to regard the Archbishop's house as his home. He was more comfortable there than in the more formidable atmosphere of the royal court.

Tensions increased between the King and Becket, and the latter went to stay at a Cistercian abbey at Pontigny. He remained there for two years, the King of France ensuring his protection and security. But eventually he had to return to England and the pace of the disagreement quickened.

It became extremely fierce when Thomas excommunicated the king for what he regarded as a serious breach of privilege. It was at this point that Henry, in great anger, uttered words that would ensure Thomas' death, although to this day no one has been able to confirm exactly what he said. The usual quote is "Will no one ride me of this turbulent priest?" Certainly, four of his knights appeared to think that they were effectively being ordered to deal with Thomas of Canterbury once and for all—to put him to the sword and thus avenge the king's honour and bring to an end a dispute that looked set to lock the country into opposing sides and possibly even bring about civil war.

Thomas' death was gruesome. He was in the cathedral, making his way to Vespers. The four knights fell on him and hacked him to death, blood gushing out on to the flagstone and pouring across the floor as they slashed at his head. He was still able to speak and was heard to say that he was prepared to die for the sake of Christ and the Church. When he was dead, the knights fled, and the cathedral clergy who had rushed to the scene found it a place of horror as blood and pieces of skull were scattered over a wide area.

Thomas was honoured as a martyr,. The king was covered with remorse. Canterbury soon became a place of pilgrimage for people from across Europe, and Henry himself came in penitence. The tomb of St Thomas of Canterbury became central to the story of Christianity in England.

The very word "Canterbury" came to be linked with "pilgrim". Geoffrey Chaucer's *Canterbury Tales*—- a collection of stories centred around a band of people making their way from London to Canterbury—are still studied today. Along the pilgrim route from

London you will find roads called "Pilgrim way" and pubs that have links going back to medieval times.

Because St Thomas Becket died in the Christmas season he became a Christmas-linked saint, with acts of charity performed in his name and Christmas celebrations evoking his story.

The poet T. S. Eliot wrote a famous play "Murder in the Cathedral" about the martyrdom of Thomas Becket. There have been numbers of books written about him. He is one of the best-known figures in English history. When Blessed John Paul came to England in 1982—we marked the 30th anniversary of his visit in 2012—he visited Canterbury, and prayed there with the Anglican primate for Christian unity.

Today, the Church in our country is free from political interference, and the Second Vatican Council emphasised the importance of religious liberty. The Church is missionary: Christianity should not be imposed as an act of the State but taught in freedom because it is the truth.

In a strange echo of names, several centuries after Thomas Becket, another Thomas and another Henry were central figures in a fresh drama. Thomas More, Chancellor of England, refused to bow to the wishes of Henry VIII and break communion with the Church in Rome. He died in 1535, executed at the king's command at London's Tower Hill.

8

St Thomas More, Chancellor of England

I F YOU VISIT the Houses of Parliament at Westminster, you will walk through the Great Hall which is the oldest part of the building. It dates back to the 11ᵗʰ century, and was built in the reign of William Rufus, the son of William the Conqueror. Many great and important events have taken place in this great hall over the centuries.

One of the grimmest events to here was the trial of Sir Thomas More. It took place here in the year 1535. Who was Thomas More? He was the Speaker of the House of Commons and Lord Chancellor of England. He was man whom many people admired, and he was known as a defender of justice and a man who wanted to serve his country to the best of his ability. So why was he put on trial?

The king at that time was King Henry VIII. He had inherited the throne from his father, Henry VII. The throne should have gone to his older brother Arthur, but he died and so young Henry became the heir instead. At the start of his reign, he was young and handsome and very popular. He married Catherine, a princess from Aragon in Spain. The plan had originally been for her to marry Arthur, and they had a wedding ceremony together, but had never lived together as man and wife because he went back to Wales and died there, before they were ever able to have a proper home together. So some years later Catherine married Henry. At first they were very happy. They had a little daughter whom they named Mary. But their other children all died as small babies. It was a sad time, as year after year went by and the sorrow increased. And Henry also got angry. He needed a son who would be king after him. He decided to abandon Catherine and marry someone else—a girl named Anne Boleyn.

No one can just announce that they want to abandon a husband or wife and marry some one new. Marriage is for life. It binds a man and a woman together to form a new family. That is God's original plan. King Henry wrote to the Pope saying that he wanted to abandon Catherine: but the Pope could not allow him to do so. The Pope and the Church can only uphold what is true about marriage. Henry and Catherine were married, and marriage lasts until death.

So Henry decided just to take charge himself. He announced that as King he was now head of the Church: the throne and the altar must always be united and that was that. People were frightened: they knew that Jesus Christ had not appointed kings to be the head of the Church, but Peter the fisherman, and all the Popes who have followed him one by one down all the ages.

King Henry ordered all the important men in England to sign a statement agreeing with his new plan. Many signed, but Sir Thomas More would not. He thought and prayed about it. He wanted to help the king, but he knew that Jesus Christ established just one Church and that no one could break away and decide to form a branch of it alone and announce that this was the true version.

Eventually, Sir Thomas More was imprisoned in the Tower of London. His wife and daughter came to see him. They, and all his family, were terrified about what might happen to him. They had been a very happy and united family: they had a large pleasant home at Chelsea, by the river Thames, and the king had even visited them there, and walked with Sir Thomas in the garden, talking and laughing and relaxing. The family home was a place of books and music, with a warm welcome for visitors. Sir Thomas began every day by going to Mass in the local church. He gave a good education to all his children, and set an example of cheerful service to everyone. It seemed terrible that all this was to end in imprisonment, or worse.

Henry married Anne Boleyn, but it was not to be a happy union. They had a baby but it was not the boy he had longed for, but another girl, Elizabeth. His defiance of the Church and the Pope had not brought him what he wanted.

What happened to Sir Thomas More? He was brought to Westminster Hall for trial on a charge of treason. No one could produce any evidence: he had never tried to make any trouble for the king and had always been loyal. He loved his country and he served it very well, upholding justice and working with others in Parliament seeking peace and prosperity. The only issue at stake was that of the king's marriage. But Thomas More was convicted of treason, and sentenced to be put to death.

No one believed he was a traitor. In June 1535 he was taken from the Tower of London to the execution block—you can still see the place—where a great crowd

had gathered. He told them "I die the king's good
servant—but God's first". He had said his prayers and
although he did not want to die he was not afraid. He
even joked with the headsman. Then, when directed,
he laid his head on the block. Then the headsman
swung the axe and Thomas More was killed.

People knew that something terrible had happened,
and that England had lost a great and noble man. King
Henry knew it, too. He was angry with Anne Boleyn,
angry with his country, angry with himself. He sent
Anne to the Tower of London and had her head
chopped off, too. He married another lady, Jane Sey-
mour, and they had a baby boy, but poor Queen Jane
died after giving birth and the boy was frail and sickly.
Henry went on to marry three more times. By the time
he died, people lived in fear of him. All the hope and
joy of the early years of his reign had vanished.

Today, Sir Thomas More is a saint of the Church—
Saint Thomas More. There is a plaque on the floor of
Westminster Great Hall where he stood trial. In 2010
Pope Benedict XVI came to England, and he spoke to
a great gathering of people in the Hall. It was a
moment of history: trumpets sounded, everyone
cheered and applauded. The Pope reminded everyone
of the importance of remembering the great moral
truths, and of allowing a nation to flourish through
this. He also spoke about St Thomas More, and as he
left the hall through crowds of cheering people, he was
shown the plaque on the floor marking where Thomas
More had stood all those long years before.

St Thomas More was a great statesman, a man of
courage and faith, some one whose life and example
have inspired many. He is the patron saint of states-
men and politicians. Britain is very proud of him.

9

St Edmund Campion, tortured but unbroken

BORN IN 1540, Edmund Campion would live in a grim and frightening time in English history. But he started life with many advantages, being educated at Christ's Hospital school and at St John's College, Oxford. He was a brilliant scholar, and by all accounts a popular person—people enjoyed his company, his great sense of humour, his gift for friendship, his loyalty. He was the outstanding scholar of his year and was chosen to give a welcoming speech in Latin when Queen Elizabeth I visited Oxford in 1553. It was an unforgettable day—the scene was a glittering one, and Campion's speech was superb. Elizabeth never forgot it—and marked out the young man in her mind as having great promise and perhaps being able to serve in some great public office some day.

Public office for an Oxford scholar in those days meant the Church. Oxford university existed to train men for the sacred ministry. But what ministry and what Church? Henry VIII, Elizabeth's father, had broken with the Catholic Church based in Rome and announced that he, as king, was now the head of the Church in England. Since then things had gone from

bad to worse. The Church of England was, by the
1550s, clearly and formally established as something
entirely separate from Rome and the Pope, the successor of St Peter, was seen as a foreign ruler to whom
Englishmen should owe no allegiance.

Campion in due course was ordained as a deacon
in the Anglican Church—but his heart was not in it.
He was troubled. There could only be one Church:
Christ has chosen his Apostles and appointed Peter as
their leader. Every bishop since that time could trace
a line right back to the Apostles. Peter's successor lived
in Rome, and every Christian knew it. This was a living
bond with Christ, and no state Church could replace
it.

Rumours began to circulate about Campion's beliefs
and loyalties. He left Oxford and went to Ireland
where he worked as a tutor to the son of a prominent
politician, and researched and published a History of
Ireland. He thought and prayed about the question of
the Church. His mind—and it was a mind hugely
enriched by reading and study and prayer—was clear.
He must join the one true Church. In 1571 he went to
the Low Countries, became a Catholic, and enrolled at
the College established by Cardinal William Allen at
Douai. He would be ordained as a Catholic priest.

While studying—and later teaching—at Douai
Campion also came to an important decision about his
spiritual allegiance. He didn't just seek to be a Catholic
priest—he wanted to join the new order founded by
Ignatius of Loyola, the Jesuits. He went to Rome and
was ordained as a Jesuit, a member of the Society of
Jesus. There followed six years as a teacher, working
mostly in Prague, And then the great mission to
England was launched, and Campion returned to his

native land. The English mission was one of the most dangerous missions that a Jesuit, or any priest, could undertake. It would cost Campion his life.

England by now was virtually a police state. The Church of England epitomised a new national identity: Elizabeth was conscious that as the daughter of the king's dalliance with Ann Boleyn she had what might be regarded as a weak claim to the throne She knew that she needed to consolidate her power. The Catholic Church was her enemy—not so much because of its doctrines or its liturgy (her father had attended Mass daily, and opposed any attempt to change it), but simply because of the bond with the successor of St Peter. It was the Catholic Church which had insisted that her father was married to Queen Catherine, his loyal spouse of many years, and thus that he could not marry Ann Boleyn. And if Henry and Ann were not married, where was Elizabeth's claim to the throne?

The Church of England was an instrument of state. People were forced to accept its doctrines and attend services in the churches of the land as a way of ensuring their loyalty to the nation and the state. It did not represent a faith renewed or freshly inspired—but rather an instrument of power, a focus of local and national unity that must not be opposed.

The Jesuit mission to England did not seek to engage with any political issues or debate the status of the Queen. It was a mission to souls, purely and simply: to teach the Catholic Faith in all its fullness, to bring the Mass and the Sacraments—now banned by law—to the people. The men embarking for England were priests of God, not political agents. But they knew they would be hunted down, and if arrested, possibly tortured, and certainly imprisoned. If they were found guilty of being Catholic priests, they would be executed—by the horrific method of hanging, drawing, and quartering.

Campion feared that he lacked the necessary courage for the mission. But he embarked on his work with great zeal. With a small group, he crossed the Channel, disguised as a jewel merchant. Contact was made with Catholic groups in London. At an early stage, he was urged by a group of leading Catholic laymen to produce a pamphlet—the printing-press, a new invention, was now crucial in the religious debates of the day—to explain his mission, emphasising that all he sought was to teach the truths of the Church, the glorious message of Christ and his saving work, offered to mankind through the Mass and the sacraments. Campion wrote brilliantly, and preached powerfully. Once his booklet began to circulate, he was very much a hunted man: the authorities knew that he could awaken consciences and stir hearts. But he went from place to place in disguise—across Berkshire and Northamptonshire and into Lancashire. He was sheltered by Catholic families, and he heard many confessions, celebrated Mass and distributed Holy Communion, taught people, baptised their children, and encouraged them to remain steadfast.

He was finally captured at Lyford Grange in Berkshire, not far from the Catholic house at Stonor where a secret printing press had been established which had produced another booklet by Campoion—his "Ten Reasons" explaining why the newly-established Anglican Church was not part of the one united true church established by Christ and flourishing under the leadership of Peter's successor in Rome.

Tied to a horse, his arms pinioned, Campion was taken to London. Here the horror began. He was brutally tortured. Elizabeth wanted him as her new Archbishop of Canterbury. Surely he would break and come to see that he had a great the glittering future in the new state Church? He would not, and thus the torture began. He was so famous that it seemed crucial to get him to recant. Ill, exhausted, and wounded by brutal torture on the rack, Campion was brought to debate with some of the leading figures of the state Church. They had books and Bibles, were relaxed and rested and prepared. Campion was sick and physically broken. But the arguments he gave and the spirit in which he gave them so impressed those watching that the debate was not repeated — Campion was generally held to have won. Among those touched and impressed was a young nobleman, Philip Howard, heir to the Duke of Norfolk. In due course he would become a Catholic and die as a martyr in the Tower of London.

At his trial, in Westminster Hall, Campion spoke stirringly and movingly, pointing out that all that he taught as a priest was all that English men and women had believed for centuries. So "in condemning us, you condemn all your own ancestors". The Faith had produced saints and scholars and centuries of Christian life "all that was once the glory of England". Posterity would judge those who were now judging the Catholic missionaries. No one forgot his words, which were later printed and circulated. The brilliant scholar of Oxford was speaking to his countrymen, and having an influence of a breadth and depth that Elizabeth could not have imagined, in circumstances at once grim and heroic.

Finally, Campion and his companions were sentenced to death. Dragged through the streets of London on a hurdle, his head under the horse's tail so that manure would drop on him, Campion was taken to Tyburn—where Marble Arch now stands. Here he was brutally hung, drawn, and quartered. His companions in death were two more heroes—Alexander Briant and Ralph Sherwin. All died with immense courage. It was 1 December 1581. They were heroes of their country and of their generation, and heroes of the Church. All three are now honoured as saints, named as among the great English Martyrs.

10

St Damien of Molokai, hero of the forgotten

AMIEN DE VEUSTER was born in Belgium and is honoured there as a national hero. But he will always be identified with a place on the other side of the world—Molokai, in Hawaii. Ordained a priest in 1860, Fr Damien prayed that he would be allowed to become a missionary. His brother, also a priest, was originally chosen for this but could not go because of illness. So Fr Damien went in his place to Hawaii, arriving at the Catholic Mission in North Kohala in 1865. The work there was tough—travel to remote villages was difficult, conditions were primitive, communication with the wider world depended on ships carrying mail. But what was to come was tougher. The Bishop called for volunteers to go to the leper colony at Molokai.

At that time, there was no known cure for leprosy—today known as Hansen's disease—and it was also thought to be highly contagious. The government of Hawaii had passed a law establishing that known sufferers should be separated from their homes and families and live together in a remote region. Molokai could only be reached by sea or by mule over a range of mountains.

At Molokai, the plan had originally been that people would build themselves homes and grow food. But this was impossible—the terrain was tough and the people were ill. Supplies were slow to arrive, and there was no proper leadership. Father Damien arrived to find drunkenness, misery, and a complete lack of hope. Most of the people were living in shacks, without basic amenities. He slept his first night under a tree and the next day he set to work with the local people.

Fr Damien introduced himself to everyone. There was no effective local leadership and people had essentially given up hope. Fr Damien began by doing what he could. He offered basic medical care, dressing the hideous sores created by the disease and helping people to look after themselves and to keep clean. He built a church, and celebrated Mass there every day, welcoming anyone and everyone. He visited people in their poor huts and gradually got these rebuilt so that they resembled decent homes. He formed a choir and got people singing. And he cared for the children, who had been running wild with no arrangements made for their education or their future. He created a school for them and, for those who had already lost their parents, a home where they could know that they were safe.

Some of the people at Molokai were in the early stages of the disease: they were beginning to experience numbness in their limbs or spots on their skin, but could live reasonably normally, working and looking after themselves. Others showed the ravages of the illness, with rotting wounds caused by untreated sores. Some were confined to bed and had been living in terrible squalor: Fr Damien gave special care to these and longed for the day when he could build a properly equipped hospital and explore possible cures and treatments.

The changes at Molokai were steady and dramatic. The drunkenness and wild behaviour had been a result of people's complete lack of any structure in their lives, and of any hope in the future. Now they had a meaning and purpose. Fr Damien lived among them, sharing food with them and treating them with warmth and friendliness. This was in great contrast to the approach taken by most people with regard to leprosy—it was believed (inaccurately) that the disease could be transmitted by mere touch, by a handshake or the sharing of a cup or plate.

Fr Damien's only contact with the rest of the world over the next years was when a ship arrived in the harbour. Visitors came from his religious order. He was able to send letters home and in due course people began to gather support for him and arrange for medical aid and other materials to arrive. By now, Molokai had begun to resemble a civilised community: music played a big part in people's lives, there were celebrations of special events, the children were being educated, the church was the daily focal point of prayer and community life.

But by this time something else had occurred: when he accidentally got boiling water on his foot but felt no pain, Damien realised that he too had contracted leprosy. Undeterred, he redoubled his efforts for his people, so that they would have a secure future after he was gone.

Because of the fear of contagion, even his talks with visitors who arrived by ship were now curtailed. When he wanted to go to confession, he had to do it by going near the ship and shouting out to a priest who stood on the deck.

By now the wonderful changes on Molokai were beginning to be known. Word of his efforts had spread, and a member of the Hawaiian royal family, Princess Lydia Lili'uokalani, came to present Damien with a medal. She was so moved by what she saw that she spent the next months and years raising funds and support for the work, and Damien became known across the world. Funds were raised in his native Belgium, and in America, and also Britain through the Church of England. Best of all, supporters and helpers arrived, including a nun, Sister Marianne Cope, who would soon be running a hospital at Molokai.

Damien sought not only to relieve the sufferings of lepers, but also to find a cure for the disease, and he worked closely with a Dr. Masanao Goto whose system of nourishing food and massages did seem to bring much relief. When Damien's own symptoms became acute, he went to Honolulu to receive treatment too.

Fr Damien died on 15 April 1889. He was 49 years old. He was buried at Molokai, under the same tree where he had slept on his first night. Much later, his body was transferred back to his native Belgium. He was canonised by Pope Benedict XVI in 2009 in a ceremony in Rome attended by the king and queen of the Belgians. Today, sufferers from Hansen's disease can receive treatment that enables them to live normal lives, and the old prejudices about the disease are disappearing. They do not need to feel that their lives are hopeless. Medical research has found all sorts of information that has brought great breakthroughs in knowledge and understanding about the disease. In the future, no one need suffer as the people on Molokai did. Fr Damien's heroic courage changed not only the lives of people there, but huge numbers of people all over the world.

11

BLESSED JOHN HENRY NEWMAN, LEADING PEOPLE TO THE LIGHT

OHN HENRY NEWMAN was a scholar, the founder of a school and a university, the author of many books, a man of great learning. But he was also something of a hero, making difficult decisions of conscience and holding fast to the search for the truth even when it brought him sorrow and hardship.

He was born in 1801 and his life spanned almost the whole of the nineteenth century, as he died in 1890. In his late teens, he experienced a profound religious conversion, and from that time on he sought to live as a sincere Christian. He studied at Oxford, and was eventually elected a Fellow of Oriel College. He was ordained in the Church of England and began parish work while continuing research and study.

Through his reading of the Church Fathers—those writers from the early centuries of the Church who expressed the beliefs of the early Christians and showed how the Church defended and upheld these— he came to see that the form of Christianity that he had been taught was inadequate. He began to seek out that original form of the "Church" that the Fathers knew: where was it to be found?

A tour of Southern Europe brought him into contact with the Catholic Church. But he was not much impressed, finding some of the sights and images jarring. On the journey home he became very ill and almost died—as he slowly recovered he had a deep sense that his life had been spared because God had some very specific work that he was meant to do in England. When he set sail to return home the ship was becalmed: in those days ships were powered by sails, which needed wind. During the long time of waiting, he wrote a hymn "Lead, kindly light" which has since become much loved, with its message of trusting in God's guidance when the future seems difficult and unclear.

Back in Oxford, Newman began a long association with what came to be called the "Oxford Movement", which developed a more Catholic understanding of the Church of England. His sermons at the University church of St Mary's became very popular. He also worked with dedication in the parish of Littlemore, a poor area outside of the city where he built a church— his mother laid the foundation stone and his sister helped with caring for local families facing sickness or poverty. Newman worked hard among the poor families, opening up a little school, and bring a sense of hope to what had been a place of real rural poverty.

As he continued to study the Fathers and the history of Christianity, Newman became convinced of the reality of a Church speaking with authority and associated always with the Bishop of Rome, the Pope. Meanwhile his "Tracts for the Times" explored crucial issues concerning the Church and made him a central figure in the religious debates of the day.

Eventually, Newman resigned from the University Church and went to live at Littlemore in a small study-centre that he had created there. It was at Littlemore that he was received into the Roman Catholic church one wet and stormy night by Dominic Barberi, an Italian missionary priest known for his zeal, poverty and holiness who had travelled to Littlemore after receiving a message that Newman wanted to see him.

As a Catholic, Newman began a new chapter of his life. He was never to return to Oxford, and he found a refuge at a house owned by a Catholic family in the countryside on Old Oscott Hill outside the new industrial city of Birmingham. He and a small group of companions were given this as a home and he named it "Maryvale". They walked over the meadows to Mass in Birmingham. In due course he studied in Rome and was ordained as a Catholic priest. He found in the idea of the Oratory established by St Philip Neri something that deeply appealed, and he was eventually able to establish one in Birmingham. A start was made in an old gin distillery—the teaching and the spiritual care was strong and attractive, and numbers attending grew and grew. Land was acquired on the Hagley Road and the Oratory Church and house built there—this was to remain Newman's base for the rest of his life.

The Oratory served many of Birmingham's poorest people as well as the emerging Catholic middle class. It was a very different way of life from the one that Newman had known in the academic life of Oxford. In addition to the vigorous parish life he founded what was to become a thriving and well-known school for boys—it still thrives as The Oratory School, near Reading—and he was asked to take on the huge task of establishing a Catholic University in Ireland. This took up a great deal of his time and energy, not least because it involved in travelling to Dublin by rail and sea.

He also became involved in a number of controversies. Many people had not really understood why he had become a Catholic, and one well-known writer attacked him savagely suggesting that he was dishonest and that the Church allowed him to be so. Newman's response was to set out the whole story of his religious beliefs, in a book that was to become a classic, the *Apologia Pro Vita Sua*. He also wrote and lectured about the reality of the situation of Catholics: what they believed and why, and the misrepresentations and injustices that they often faced.

Newman's decision to follow his conscience required much courage. His ideas on the development of Christian doctrine, on the essential importance of searching for truth and the freedom necessary for this to take place, were often misunderstood within the Church. Much-loved within his Oratorian community, and by the people he served in Birmingham, he was often hurt by others and misrepresented in the press.

When he died, he was mourned by huge crowds in Birmingham, and recognised as a great figure whose writing had inspired many people and whose work would live long after him. Today we still sing his hymns, read his books, and benefit from his teaching: he greatly influenced the Second Vatican Council held by the Church in the twentieth century, and his writings on the Church Fathers meant that after centuries of neglect they became central in the education and training of priests. And he was a man of prayer: books of his prayers and meditations have helped many people to become closer to God. His spiritual journey following the "kindly light" of Christ became one that helped others to seek and find that light too.

12

St Charles Lwanga
and his companions,
Heroes of Africa

I N THE LATE nineteenth century, Christian missionaries arrived in the African country we today call Uganda. At first, the ruler, the Kabacka, was impressed and was glad to see his people acquiring some of the skills and knowledge that these people from far away had brought. But when he was succeeded by a younger ruler, things changed. The new young Kabacka began by being friendly to the missionaries, but then he became irritated by the fact that the people who were converting to Christianity seemed to be passing out of his control.

There were both Anglican and Catholic missionaries in Uganda. They made many converts. The people who became Christian had to make many sacrifices: men could no longer have several wives, for example, and they had to turn away from worshipping the old gods which had been part of the ancient traditions of their people. But they could see that in Christianity there was something that purified and brought out the best in all the long history of their people: it was as if this was something for which generations had been waiting and waiting.

Among those who converted to Christianity were many of the pages at the court of the young Kabacka. These pages came from the country's leading families. They were strong and energetic, skilled at hunting and at wrestling. Their families were proud of them: to serve the Kabacka at court was a great honour.

The Kabacka grew more and more irritated with the Christians. His pages went off to catechism classes. They met together to pray. Meanwhile his own life was going wrong: selfish and greedy, he lacked any true friends and he quarrelled with those who tried to help him. And against all the traditions and beliefs of his people, he had also begun to indulge in something that he and everyone else knew to be wrong—he wanted the pages to engage in homosexual acts with him.

In addition, the Christian missionaries were of course linked to European countries, which were busy colonising Africa. The Kabacka was afraid: these strong and powerful nations from far away were able to send armies and invade wherever they wanted. When an Anglican bishop, who had only peaceful intentions, came to visit the missionaries and decided to travel by an overland route, the Kabacka decided that this meant that an invasion was planned—he had the Bishop stopped and killed. When Joseph Mukasa, one of the Kabacka's chief advisers and a Catholic convert, attempted to tell him that he had done something evil in ordering this murder, the Kabacka had him killed too.

One evening, after a day's hunting had been disappointing and unsuccessful the Kabacka gave his young pages an ultimatum. They must choose: either Christianity or obeying him and serving him. One by one the pages had to go and stand with "Those who pray" or with those who did not. Bravely, all the new young converts to Christianity walked over to the Christian side. Among them was Charles Lwanga, who was the leading page of the court. Tall and athletic, he had a commanding presence, and was very popular, a natural leader and one who always showed fair play and was generous and kind. He had received instruction and baptism from the White Fathers—so named because of their long white robes—and then in turn had given instruction to the other pages, explaining the Faith and answering their questions. He had brought them along to the Fathers for further instruction and for baptism.

Most of these pages who now bravely affirmed their faith were thus very new converts. They did not have catechisms or books. They had been taught about God the Father, and his Son, Jesus Christ, about his Virgin Mother Mary and his birth at Bethlehem, about his miracles, about the Last Supper and Calvary and his Resurrection and Ascension. They knew about Pentecost and about the Holy Spirit. They had never seen a great cathedral or heard the glorious music of a Mozart Mass sung by a famous choir. They had only just begun to learn the cycle of feasts and seasons in the Church's calendar and to know about the heritage of centuries of saints and martyrs. Their "yes" to Christ was given with great courage.

Chained and marched through the jungle, denied rest and water, the young pages eventually arrived at Namugongo, a traditional site of execution. Their death would be watched by a large crowd, and the grisly ceremonies began with witch-doctors dancing with a ritual chant, calling out "The mothers of these will weep today—yes, they will weep today". Some of the boys' families begged and pleaded with them to renounce their faith and save their lives. Meanwhile a great stack of wood was being prepared for a ritual fire.

One of the youngest boys was named Kitzito. He was terrified and shaking with fear, but he still refused to renounce his new-found faith in Christ. He told Charles Lwanga of his fears, and Charles promised him that they would face things together, and that he would not be alone.

The boys were taken to the fire, and wrapped in rush mats and hurled on to the flames. When it was Kitzito's turn, he called out that he was not afraid, and he began to sing a hymn in a clear and strong voice.

Charles Lwanga was the last to die: the Kabacka had ordered that he must be made to watch all the others die first, and that that he must be burned very slowly so as to prolong the agony.

It was June 1886, and Ascension Day. All those watching knew that what was happening would never be forgotten. They heard the boys calling out in prayer, saying the "Our Father" even as the flames leapt around them. Some of them also called out that they were not in pain, that they felt as though cool water was running over them.

Some weeks before, Charles Lwanga had been trying to arrange for a special celebration for Easter with the missionary fathers, and it had not been possible: "But we will have a proper celebration for Ascension Day" he said. Now, this day was to be the day he would actually meet Christ in Heaven.

Today, Uganda is a Christian country. The martyrs of Uganda are honoured, and their feast-day every June sees huge crowds gathered at Namugongo, where

Mass is celebrated with choirs and music and great ceremony. The churches in Uganda are full, and priests are sent from there to be missionaries back in Britain and other countries in Europe. The courage and faith of St Charles Lwanga and his companions achieved something far greater than the Kabacka could ever have imagined.

13

FATHER WILLIE DOYLE, HERO OF THE TRENCHES

HE FIRST WORLD War was a tragedy that mapped out a whole new set of miseries that would mark the rest of the twentieth century. But when it broke out in the summer of 1914 it did not seem that way at all: young men in Britain rallied to join the Army: there was a great sense of adventure, and a great idealism and a desire to serve the country and to defend the great things that Britain represented.

Britain in 1914 was an extraordinarily beautiful country: no motorways or electricity pylons, no tall skyscraper office blocks. There were large noisy cities, a great deal of poverty, swathes of glorious country-side, very pretty towns and villages, an extremely good railway network, and an emerging sense of excitement as a new century got under way which people felt would be one of progress and human flourishing. The nineteenth century had seen great developments in medicine, and life expectancy was lengthening. Churches flourished and with them a great range of social welfare groups of various kinds. People felt that, although Britain was not perfect, it was a wonderful country—and it ruled a great Empire that included India, Australia, much of Africa, and more. They believed that all this was worth defending, and they believed that it was in some way under threat by the events that were unfolding in Europe, and that Germany was in danger of trampling on smaller European nations and that Britain ought to defend these.

It was with a great sense of idealism that many young men went to war. And many were expecting adventures and possibilities for heroism. No one could have foreseen the horrible reality of trench warfare with weeks spent living in holes dug in the ground surrounded by mud, filth, and dead bodies. None could foresee that the war would topple thrones, usher in the Russian Revolution that would impose misery on millions, and create new uncertainties across Europe that would result in another war within two decades.

A young priest went to war with the British Army as a chaplain. He was an Irishman, Willie Doyle, born in 1873 in Dalkey, Co. Dublin, one of seven children from a well-to-do family. At that time, Ireland formed part of the United Kingdom. Irishmen went off to join the British Army in large numbers. A dedicated priest, Father Doyle knew that these young soldiers needed a chaplain. He had already chosen a path of complete dedication to God. As a child he had denied himself cakes and sweets in Lent, and as a young Jesuit novice he willingly took of the nastiest jobs in the house and volunteered cheerfully for anything that seemed difficult or tiresome.

'By entering religion and taking my vows I have given myself over absolutely to God and His service' he wrote. 'He, therefore, has a right to be served in the way he wishes. If then he asks me to enter on a hard, mortified life and spend myself working for him, how can I resist his will and desire? O my God, make me a saint and I consent to suffer all you ask for the rest of my life. What is God asking from me now? Shall I go back on that offering?'

Father Willie never went back. As a military chaplain he was appointed to the Royal Irish Fusiliers, of the 16th (Irish) Division. The Western Front was now a battlefield where many were dying every day. He saw his task as being with his men whenever they needed him, to be the presence of God and the Church for them: to hear confessions, to celebrate Mass, to bring Holy Communion to the wounded and sick, to anoint the dying even in the heat of battle without regard for his own safety. He was at the Battle of Loos in April 1916 when the use of poison gas caused many casualties, and at the bitter fighting in August at Ginchy and Guillemont. He risked his life again and again to help rescue the wounded under fire, or to anoint men as they lay on the battlefield. The men loved him: he was unfailingly courageous and always reliable: they knew he was always with them. He was cheerful and hard-working. He took on any unpleasant chore with goodwill. He wrote letters for the wounded, helped men to send and receive news from home, stayed with the wounded when they were in pain or great fear. He made it clear to the men that their souls mattered: they were beloved of God—if they were to die, they had a home waiting for them in Heaven and they needed to be ready for this. He wanted them to go into battle with clean souls: they went to confession to him and received Holy Communion at his hands, and they knew that if death came he would be there to pray for them and if possible to anoint them and give them the comfort of the last rites.

Because of his courage under fire, Father Doyle received the Military Cross in January 1917. In August of that year he was killed in a shell attack at Frezenberg Ridge. He was 34 years old.

The military records show that in addition to his Military Cross—awarded for acts of outstanding bravery—Fr Doyle was also recommended for a DSO and also for the Victoria Cross, Britain's highest military honour, awarded for acts of supreme valour. There were complicated political considerations against awarding too many high medals to an Irish Catholic priest—and a Jesuit—at that time, which is probably why the medals were not awarded. But he had in any case become a legend in the British Army for his courage and his fearlessness, and his utter dedication to his men. They always said that he showed a total disregard for his own safety. In his letters home he made light of this saying that he was a coward but that "when duty calls I know I can count on the help of the One who has never failed me yet."

At his death, his family was overwhelmed with letters and messages from men he had helped, and from the families of those to whom he had ministered when they were dying. All spoke of his courage, kindness, cheerfulness in the face of great hardships, and spirit of service. In Ireland, he became something of a national hero.

A chaplain of the First World War seems remote from us now. But Father Willie Doyle has not been forgotten and it has been suggested that the cause for his beatification and eventual canonisation be put forward. Books and magazine articles continue to be written about him, and his story continues to inspire young priests.

Some years after his death, his father was woken in the night by a burglar in the house. The man was rifling through the drawers and cupboards. He stopped short at a small picture of Father Willie that stood on a shelf and asked who it was. "That is my son, Father Willie Doyle, who gave his life for the soldiers in Flanders" Mr Doyle told him. The thief took up the card and kissed it. "That was a holy priest. He saved many souls" he said, and left the house with the card in his hand, taking nothing else at all.

14

BLESSED RUPERT MAYER, SOLDIER AND SAINT

UPERT MAYER WAS a man of immense talents — a musician, a sportsman, a brilliant student — who chose to dedicate his life to God as a Catholic priest and is today honoured as a saint and a hero among his fellow-Germans. Born in Stuttgart in 1876, he was ordained in 1899 and the next year joined the Jesuit Order. Over the next years, he worked with dedication as a priest in Munich, caring in particular for the needs of people who had come to the city looking for work. He showed them that as they settled in a strange city they should not feel remote from God: the Church was there and should be at the centre of their lives. He organised programmes of practical help for poor families, with gifts of food and clothing when necessary. He helped people to find jobs and supported them in difficulties. Above all, he taught them the Faith, celebrated Mass for them and brought them the sacraments.

When the First World War broke out in 1914 he immediately volunteered to serve in a field-hospital at the battle-front. In due course he served with soldiers in numerous battles, with them in the front-line and sharing every risk and danger. He heard men's confessions, celebrated Mass in the battle-zone, took the Blessed Sacrament to wounded men, and anointed the dying at the risk of his own life. He was awarded the Iron Cross—a high decoration for outstanding bravery—in 1915. The following year, he was badly injured and his badly broken leg had to be amputated. The stump would cause him problems for the rest of his life, but he never complained.

The war's end in 1918 saw Germany impoverished and with a bleak future. Father Mayer, with no concern for his own injuries, set to work to help people in Munich. He established a men's sodality dedicated to Our Lady which had branches across the city, involving him in the leadership of some 70 groups for which he had care. He worked to help poor families and to establish voluntary groups providing for people's practical needs. One idea which was a big success was the celebration of Mass at railway stations very early in the morning on summer Sundays, so that families could fulfil their religious obligations while having a day out—this meant that he was often at the station by 3 am to prepare for the first Mass for people catching an early train.

Father Mayer became one of the most popular figures in Munich—a beacon of hope at a time of much political confusion and economic uncertainty.

The National Socialist Party was rising in power and influence, and Father Mayer saw how its ideas were becoming popular. He attended their meetings and talked to the young people. Recognising their genuine fears and hopes for the future, he challenged them about the Nazi ideology. At that time, many people felt that the Nazi ideas could fit together with Christian beliefs, but Father Mayer showed that this was impossible. The central Christian beliefs about the dignity of every human being, the importance of God's law, and the value of human solidarity irrespective of race clashed with National Socialism again and again.

When the Nazis started closing Catholic schools and criticising the Church Father Mayer preached against them. In 1937 the now-powerful Nazi government banned him from speaking in public places. But it could not silence him in his own church, and he continued to denounce Nazism from the pulpit. Because he was a popular priest and a war hero, people listened to him and valued what he had to say. He became a real danger to the Nazi regime.

At one stage, Father Mayer was arrested but later released after a short term in prison. But in 1940—with Germany now at war—he was arrested again and sent to a concentration camp. He was 63 years old, crippled and ill. Conditions in the camp—the Oranienberg-Sachsenhausen camp near Germany's capital, Berlin—were grim, and his condition rapidly worsened. The Nazi authorities were worried that he would die. As an extremely well-known and popular priest, already wounded in his country's service, he would be regarded as a martyr. They could not risk that. He was released and sent to live in an abbey in the Alpine region of Bavaria. His health was poor and his life was very restricted. The censored newspapers wrote nothing about him, and with wartime travel very difficult, people were unable to visit him. He seemed to disappear from view.

But in 1945, as the war was ending, the American forces rushing across Bavaria reached the Abbey. Father Mayer was returned to Munich—and the people there quickly learned of his arrival and gave him a hero's welcome. They were living in the ruins of their city, bombed out of their homes and finding shelter wherever they could, struggling to find food and fearful of the future. Many of the men were missing, killed, or prisoners-of-war far away. The children were hungry. Many of the city's main buildings and landmarks had been destroyed. Undeterred by his own ill-health, Father Mayer immediately set to work to try to help people.

On 1 November, he celebrated Mass for the feast of All Saints in St Michael's church. As he started to preach the sermon, he had a sudden heart attack. His last words were "The Lord... the Lord... " and then he collapsed and died.

Initially buried in a cemetery just outside the city, Rupert Mayer's body was later brought back to the Burgersaal church in the city centre. He had often celebrated Mass there, and led the men's sodality which met there.

People visited his grave regularly to pray and left candles and flowers there, asking Rupert Mayer to pray for them. In 1987, in a great ceremony in Munich, Pope John Paul declared him Blessed. On a visit to the city in 2005, Pope Benedict XVI prayed at the grave: as a Bavarian himself, he had a special closeness to Rupert Mayer and his parents had been strong supporters and admirers of him.

Blessed Rupert Mayer was a wounded war hero who was unafraid to tell his countrymen the truth about what was happening. He was not deterred by imprisonment or suffering, and he showed by his own example that priesthood is about service. He used his energy and talents not to make money for himself or bask in personal success but to serve others. At a time when his country was in a state of moral confusion, he taught that Christian moral values must always remain central—and that this may require courage. Today, his grave is a place of pilgrimage, and the message of his life gives hope and inspiration to a new generation of young Germans, who must live the Christian faith amid the new challenges of the twenty-first century.

15

EMPEROR KARL, SOLDIER AND PEACEMAKER

 RCHDUKE KARL VON Habsburg was born into one of the great ruling families of Europe. But at his birth it was not expected that he would become ruler of the Habsburg Austro-Hungarian empire. He was a comparatively minor Archduke. A series of extraordinary events including the shooting of his uncle, Franz-Ferdinand, meant however that he inherited the throne of Austria-Hungary in 1916, in the middle of a terrible war.

Karl spoke the various different languages of the Empire, which brought together people from territories as diverse as Poland and Hungary, parts of Northern Italy and the Czech and Slovak lands. As a young man, when became clear that he was to become heir to the throne he dedicated himself to training in statecraft, making himself familiar with politics and current affairs with great seriousness. He knew very well that not everyone in central and Eastern Europe was happy with Habsburg rule—many of these lands really wanted more independence. Karl himself believed that it was wrong to try to keep the Empire together in a rigid way. He believed that a looser federation was required, with people having their own local systems of governance, and with ties of trade and goodwill between each other. It was tragic, however, that he would never get the chance to put these ideas into practice: he inherited the throne in the middle of a terrible war.

Karl was essentially a man of peace. He was a sincere Catholic and understood that government was about service, with a special concern for the poor and the vulnerable. He was a man of prayer, and his own personal lifestyle was centred on family life, the countryside and simple pleasures. He had a good grasp of history and no pretentious ideas about his rights and privileges, but rather a genuine desire to accept the responsibilities that he had been given.

He had served as a soldier and knew what war really meant. He believed with his whole heart that his Empire must now make peace. Thousands of men were now dying every day. The war had begun because his uncle had been assassinated by a gunman linked to Serbian nationalists. But now it had spread and there was wholesale slaughter. France and Britain were lined up against Austria-Hungary and Germany. Britain had a vast overseas Empire, and men from Australia and New Zealand and Canada were now involved in the fighting in large numbers. It was truly a World War, and growing greater in scale every week.

Because of wartime conditions, Karl's coronation, in the Hungarian capital of Budapest, did not include all the grand banquets and celebrations that would normally have been held. But to many of the people in the great ceremony in the cathedral it was still a matter of pomp and pride. Not for Karl: he and his wife, the Empress Zita, prayed earnestly for peace as they knelt together. They were united by a deep conviction that God was calling them to dedicate themselves to peace with all their hearts, and to serve their people with love and humility.

Empress Zita was from the Bourbon-Parma family. They were a French Royal family living in Italy. Part of the heartbreak of World War I was that it divided families. While Zita was Empress in Austria, her two brothers were with the Belgian Army, fighting on the other side. But they were all still in touch with one another, and the bonds of love and trust were strong. With great secrecy, in early 1917, a meeting was arranged and Prince Sixtus, the Empress' brother, came to Laxenburg Castle in Austria. A peace-plan was hammered out. Emperor Karl would propose negotiations based on this plan. Essentially, it involved giving away territory. He knew that his ally, the German Emperor, would be very angry if the plans were discovered and would try to stop everything: in both Germany and Austria there were many in top government positions who believed that the war could be won and that the fighting should continue until a ruthless victory had been obtained.

Tragically, the French and the British did not respond to the peace initiative. Charles was humiliated when the plan was leaked, and his position was weakened. The war continued. The death toll rose inexorably. The suffering across all of Austria-Hungary was very great. The Empire began to disintegrate under the strain.

The war ended in November 1918. By now, the Austro-Hungarian Empire was in chaos. Soldiers just wanted to return home. In a final attempt to secure some sort of negotiated peace, Karl stepped aside from the throne—although he did not formally abdicate. The victorious Allies were supporting the various independence groups that were seeking to establish new nations in what had been the Empire. Karl did not want to stand in the way of peace.

Over the next two years, living in exile, Karl sought to regain his throne in Hungary. It should have worked—he had popular support and the monarchy would have been a point of unity and goodwill at a time of terrible upheaval and ethnic tensions. But there were too many people with other ambitions, and Charles had too few friends abroad and most of the world's governments had fears and worries of their own and were not looking to support a monarch, however well-intentioned, in a complicated part of central Europe.

Karl died in exile on the island of Madeira in 1922. By now he was impoverished and ill. He caught pneumonia and there was very little money for good medical care. He and Zita had a large family—eight children—and their marriage and home life was a great consolation to them. As he lay dying, Charles blessed his unborn baby—Zita was then expecting their eighth child.

All his life, Karl had been a dedicated Catholic. He and Zita had consecrated their marriage with prayer and together had tried to serve the cause of peace. Even in his last illness, he was praying for the people of his empire and begging God to grant them relief and unity.

After his death, people spoke of Karl as the "peace emperor" and many spoke openly of him as a saint. In 2004 he was declared Blessed by Pope John Paul, who also announced that his feast-day would be 21 October, his wedding-day. He is a special patron saint for married men, fathers of families who also take responsibility in the community and in public life.

16

FATHER JOHN HAWES, THE BUILDER IN THE BUSH

N 1898 FOR the first time the Royal Academy exhibition in London, which previously had only shown paintings, invited architects to display their work in scale models. A young architect named John Hawes, who had studied at the Central School of Arts and Crafts, submitted a model of a church which attracted much interest. A Bishop in Northumberland asked him to design a church which was in due course built at Gunnerton.

Inspired by his time with Bishop Hornby, John Hawes experienced a deep Christian conversion and decided to train for ordination in the Church of England. He entered Lincoln Theological College and in due course was ordained and was appointed curate at a church in Clerkenwell in London. Later he briefly joined a religious community at Caldy Island and after leaving there he joined a missionary team established by Bishop Hornby to go to the Bahamas. A fierce hurricane there had left devastation, and in addition to ministering to the local people, Hawes was able to use his architectural skills: he repaired several churches and designed and built a church dedicated to St Paul in Clarence Town.

In 1911 he made another momentous decision: to join the Catholic Church. This meant that he had to resign his Anglican ministry. He had no immediate plans for the future and had to think things out. He travelled to New York and then on to Canada, working for a while as a labourer on the great Canadian Pacific Railway. He also worked on farms on the prairie, rounding up cattle. It was all a long way from the life of a London curate, or indeed of a student of architecture. Finally he made a decision, went to Rome and was enrolled at the Beda College. He was ordained as a Catholic priest in 1913.

A whole new set of adventures now began. In Rome, Father Hawes met Bishop William Kelly from Western Australia. His diocese of Geraldton needed more priests, and Fr Hawes willingly volunteered. It would mean living in the Australian outback and helping to build up communities there in a pioneering spirit. And Geraldton needed a cathedral, so his architectural skills would be of value. He made the long journey—it took over a month by sea in those days—from Europe to Australia.

Working in a parish in the goldfields, Father Hawes had plenty to do, but he also designed with great care what would eventually become the Cathedral of St Francis Xavier in Geraldton. It is today one of the city's most notable buildings. He also designed and built a number of other churches across Western Australia: at Mulewa, at Morawa, at Carnarvon, at Northampton, at Utakarra and at Perenjori. He was a bush priest: he lived and worked among the people he served in the mid-west of Western Australia. He didn't just design things on paper: he worked physically at building too. Today, tourists can go from place to place on the

"Monsignor Hawes trail", visiting the churches that he created. They tell the story of the building up of Catholic communities in that part of Australia in the first half of the twentieth century, long before the days of motorways, or speedy communication by email. Fr Hawes was creating Australian history—and also living it, serving the country people on the farms of Western Australia, travelling in the dust and heat, building and planning.

But Fr Hawes—he was created a Monsignor in 1937 in thanksgiving for his services to the Church—was also something of a mystic. Although an intensely practical man, he longed to live as a hermit. Finally, in 1939 after his years in the bush he left Australia and returned to the Bahamas. Here he settled as a hermit on Cat Island. He took the name Fra Jerome. But people still needed him and his building skills. The local people begged him for help, and he started to assist them in repairing churches and also in building a college, a convent and a monastery in the capital, Nassau. As always, this involved real practical work and not merely making meticulous designs on paper.

He had worked hard all his life, and in old age he was worn out. He wanted to be buried in a cave that he had specially prepared on Cat Island. In his final illness in 1956 he was given care in a hospital in Florida and then when he died on 26 June, his body was taken back to the Bahamas as he had wished. His monuments are the churches across Western Australia which are today still at the heart of the communities that worship in them, places of prayer and beauty in the towns established in the bush by pioneers.

17

THE MEXICAN MARTYRS: "VIVA CRISTO REY!"

N THE EARLY years of the twentieth century a vicious anti-Catholic campaign was launched by the Mexican government, run by the Party of the Institutional Revolution. A new Mexican Constitution forced into law in 1917 meant that all that the Mexican people had ever known and loved in their Catholic practices and traditions were banned from the public sphere. Churches had to be registered. Public teaching of the Catholic faith was blocked. Any opposition was denounced as "counter-revolutionary". Hatred of the Church was official policy. Over the next years, a great many Mexican men would die as martyrs. Many were priests, killed for celebrating Mass and for defending the rights of faithful Catholic people.

Fr Christopher Magallanes was a priest who worked hard for his people in the town of Totachihe. He founded schools, and also workshops for the young where they could learn carpentry and other skills. In an area plagued by drought, he was a leader in planning the successful building of a dam to ensure a good water supply. He helped to found a mission to the local Indian people in Azqueltan, serving the Huichol tribe.

The government's crushing of churches and schools caused widespread unrest and there were calls for armed rebellion: this eventually erupted in 1927 in the Cristeros uprising, in which large numbers of Catholic men became highly effective and courageous soldiers in a guerilla war. Father Magallanes preached against the armed struggle, believing that it would only mean worse suffering and bloodshed. Instead, he called for peaceful opposition and worked to sustain people in their faith. When the Government forcible closed the seminary in Guadalajara where men were training for the priesthood, he opened a seminary in his own parish with the support of the bishop, and it soon attracted a team of keen students.

In May 1927 Fr Magallanes went to a farm to celebrate Mass. By now it was dangerous to do this. He was risking his life and he knew it. He was arrested and denounced as a supporter of the armed rebellion against the government—even though he had publicly and strongly preached against it and was known as a supporter of peace. On his arrest, he forgave his executioners, and even gave to them his last few possessions. He was shot in the town of Colotlan, along with another priest Father Agustin Caloca. His last words were "I die innocent, and ask God that my blood may serve to unite my Mexican brethren." It was 21 May 1927

In Ocober of 1927 another priest, Fr Rodrigo Aguilar Alemán was martyred. He was known as a poet and a playwright and was a popular preacher and much loved. He was ministering to people in a rural area, working secretly from a ranch near the town of Ejutla, when he was denounced by one of the members of his own parish.

There was no trial: the day after his arrest Father Alemán was led to the main town square. He refused to show anger or hatred: he blessed his captors and gave one of them his rosary. But they didn't hang him at once: they wanted to prolong his suffering and also try to make him renounce his faith. The soldiers placed a noose around his neck and asked him "Who lives?" The correct answer was "Long live the supreme government!" But instead he gave the answer of the Cristeros: "Long live Christ the king and his Blessed Mother!" They tried again, and got the same answer— and then a third time. This final time they left him hanging until he was dead.

All of this was witnessed by the local people. They never forgot it. In the year 2000, Fathers Magallanes , Caloca and Aleman were canonised by Pope John Paul 11 along with over twenty other Mexican martyrs. Their feast-day is 21 May.

In November of 1927 another young priest, Father Miguel Pro, was martyred. He was a Jesuit, and had to be trained and ordained abroad as it was no longer possible for the Jesuits to run any seminaries or colleges in Mexico. He studied in Nicaragua—where he also taught at a school—and later in Belgium, where he was ordained. He had always suffered from poor health and was never physically strong, but always made light of this even though he had to endure various operations. In 1926 he returned to Mexico, travelling via the famous shrine for the sick at Lourdes, where he celebrated Mass.

The law in Mexico now imposed a fine for any priest wearing clerical garments in public, and five years'

imprisonment for any priest who criticised the government. In some parts of the country, notably the state
of Tabasco, all the churches were closed. Priests could
only operate secretly, saying Mass in private homes,
travelling from place to place. Father Pro became one
of these heroic priests, living without a permanent
home, never knowing when he might be arrested,
staying in safe houses and bringing people the Sacraments secretly. At one point he was arrested, and kept
in prison for a short while but later released. He was
a marked man.

In November 1927 after an assassination attempt on
the President, Fr Pro was arrested again. He had had
no involvement whatever with the assassination and
those who were involved in it had made this clear. He
was not given a trial. Late at night on 22 November he
was taken to a cell. The next morning, he was led out
to be shot. H showed no fear, and blessed the soldiers
as they lined up to form a firing-squad. He knelt down
and prayed, a rosary in one hand and a crucifix in the
other. As he finished his prayer, he called out to the
soldiers: "May God have mercy on you! May God bless
you! Lord, Thou knowest that I am innocent! With all
my heart I forgive my enemies!" Finally, he stood up,
ready to face the firing-squad. He was offered a
blindfold but refused. He stood calmly, and opened
wide his arms in the form of a cross. Then he shouted
the great cry of the Cristeros: "Viva Cristo Rey!" -"Long
live Christ the King!"

The shots of the firing-quad failed to kill Fr Pro, and
so one of the soldiers quickly went to him and shot
him at point-blank range.

The government forces had photographed Fr Pro as
he stood facing the firing-squad. Perhaps they thought

that reports of his death would frighten people into submission and end the Cristeros war. But the reverse happened. At Fr Pro's funeral no priest was allowed. But 40,000 people came, and stood with his family as his father pronounced the Church's traditional prayers. Many carried newspaper pictures of Fr Pro standing with his arms outstretched. It is possibly the only time that a saint has been photographed at the very moment of martyrdom.

Fr Pro was beatified in September 1988 and he is now Blessed Miguel Pro. At his Beatification, Pope John Paul said: "Neither suffering nor serious illness, neither the exhausting ministerial activity, frequently carried out in difficult and dangerous circumstances, could stifle the radiating and contagious joy which he brought to his life for Christ and which nothing could take away. Indeed, the deepest root of self-sacrificing surrender for the lowly was his passionate love for Jesus Christ and his ardent desire to be conformed to him, even unto death."

Fathers Magallanes, Caloca, Aleman, and Pro are just three of the great host of heroic Mexican martyrs from the 1920s. After the Cristeros war finally came to an end with a negotiated settlement, which the Government did not fully honour, Catholics continued to face all sorts of restrictions on the public celebration of their faith. But today, in the 21st century, the Church in Mexico is free and is thriving. The martyrs and the heroes of the Cristeros are honoured and their courage inspires young people of a new generation.

18

St Maximilian Kolbe, martyr for charity

Raymond Kolbe was born in 1894 in a part of Poland which at that time belonged to the Russian empire. He was one of a family of boys. In 1907, along with his brother Francis he wanted to become a Franciscan Friar. This was not possible in the Russian part of Poland so they had to cross—illegally—to the part that was ruled by Austria. Here they joined the junior seminary at Lwow, and when he made his vows as a monk Raymond took the name Maximilian Maria. All his life he was to have a special devotion to Mary, the mother of Christ.

He was sent to study in Rome, and while he was there he saw big demonstrations organised against the Pope and the Church, and he vowed to win over these people to Christ and to Mary. He founded the *Militia Immaculata,* or Army of Mary—the battles they would fight would be spiritual and the aim was to convert people to a good Christian way of life. In Rome Father Maximilian also obtained his doctorate in theology, and was ordained a priest.

He returned to Poland and there his Friars of the Immaculate grew from strength to strength. Father Maximilian established a community at Niepoka-

lanów. The Friars taught the Catholic faith, emphasising devotion to Mary. They ran projects for young
people and organised retreats and conferences. They
published a newspaper—using the latest printing
technology—and it became the most widely-read
publication in Poland with thousands and thousands
of copies being printed daily. They also published a
monthly magazine, which proved even more popular
with a circulation of over a million. In 1930 Father
Maximilian was sent as a missionary to Japan. Here,
he established a big community, a seminary for training priests, and a newspaper, building a monastery in
the shelter of a great mountain, some distance from
the city centre.

When he returned to Poland six years later he
immediately became busy with the next projects at his
monastery. But war was looming. When the Nazis
invaded, Jewish people were rounded up and taken
to concentration camps where eventually millions
would be killed. Father Maximilian sheltered large
numbers of Jewish people at Niepokalanów. He and
his friars organised food and shelter for them, sharing
whatever they had. All the resources of the monastery
were put to use: eventually some 2,000 Jewish people
found a refuge there.

Father Maximilian was known to be a passionate
opponent of the Nazis. He used the monastery's radio
to tell people the truth about the evil things that the
Nazis believed and taught. He preached about the
need to speak up for truth and charity and justice.
Eventually he was arrested and sent to prison, and
from there to the big concentration camp at Auschwitz.

Father Maximilian had been brought up to be a
Polish patriot who loved his country. And first and

foremost he was a Catholic priest who loved and
served God. In Auschwitz all that he had loved seemed
to be in ruins: Poland was occupied by enemy troops
and people were imprisoned, starving, and terrified.
God must have seemed far away. The Church was not
free: a monk could be arrested for teaching about love
and justice.

But it was in Auschwitz that St Maximilian Kolbe
would do the noblest of all possible things, giving up
his life for another. The camp was a cruel place, of
horror and terror. One morning it was discovered that
three men were missing: it seemed that they had
escaped. The camp commandant announced a dreadful and horrific punishment: ten men, selected at
random, would be sent to an underground bunker to
starve to death there slowly. At morning roll-call
guards walked down the lines of men and took out
one here, one there, to march them to the bunker. One
man cried out in agony and despair as he was being
led away—'My wife! My children!.' From among the
lines of men, Maximilian Kolbe stepped forward. 'I
will take his place' he said. The guard commander
could not believe what he was hearing: 'Who are you?'
he asked. 'I am a Catholic priest' was the answer 'and
I will go to the bunker in place of this man, who has a
wife and family.'

With this statement, Maximillin Kolbe began the
greatest possible witness to his priesthood—a witness
which he gave day after day, for nearly two terrible
weeks as he and his fellow-sufferers slowly died of
hunger and thirst in the underground cell. The guards
kept watch. They expected the men to be swearing and
surly, full of anger and bitterness expressed in obscen-
ities and foul language. But it was not like that: the cell

instead was filled with prayer. The men sang hymns
and prayed the Rosary. As, one by one, they died, each
was surrounded by the prayers of the others. Finally,
only Kolbe was left, lying on the floor, too weak to talk,
unable to get up. The guards wanted to finish him off
so they arrived with a syringe of sulphuric acid. He
lifted his arm and they injected it, and thus he died.

Pope Paul VI declared Maximilian Kolbe Blessed,
and Pope John Paul II canonised him. He declared him
to be 'a martyr for charity'. The Nazis had so hated
human beings that they slaughtered millions of them.
Maximilian Kolbe's heroic witness showed the Christian love of a man for his fellow men.

The man for whom Kolbe gave his life, Franciszek
Gajowniczek, went on to have a normal family life
after the war, and lived to give evidence testifying to
Kolbe's heroism and sacrifice, and to see him honoured
by the Church.

The monastery that St Maximilian Kolbe established
in Japan survived the terrible atomic bomb that
destroyed Nagasaki, and it thrives to this day. In
Poland, the Friars of the Immaculate still serve God
and Our Lady, working with young people and telling
the good news about human beings and God's great
love for us.

Today people visit Auschwitz in large numbers, and
see evidence of the terrible things that were done there,
the murder of so many Jewish people, the pitiful stacks
of their clothing and suitcases and other items that
were taken from them as they arrived, the long lists of
the dead. The underground cell where St Maximilian
Kolbe met his death is now a place of pilgrimage. It is
a grim place: a dark, terrible room with its bare walls,
its single bucket-lavatory, its dank prison smell. A

wreath of fresh flowers is now always there, and people come in to kneel and pray. Because of the heroic sacrifice of a saint of God, this is a holy place, a reminder that men are capable of great and noble things as well as terrible ones. St Maximilian Kolbe's life and witness is a bright light in the darkness of a most horrific chapter in European history.

19

BISHOP COUNT VON GALEN, THE "LION OF MUNSTER"

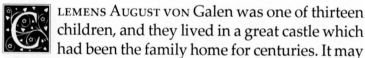

LEMENS AUGUST VON Galen was one of thirteen children, and they lived in a great castle which had been the family home for centuries. It may have seemed grand—but actually life in the castle was rather austere, as modern comforts such as central heating and comfortable bathrooms were lacking.

The children's regime was a fairly Spartan one, beginning with daily Mass at an early hour—anyone who came late to Mass got no butter on his bread at breakfast, and missing Mass meant no breakfast at all. But Count von Galen would later recall the great warmth and joy of family affection, and in middle age could be reduced to tears by hearing a hymn which his parents had loved, or taking part in a religious ceremony which brought back childhood memories.

Educated partly at home and partly at a Jesuit boarding school, the young Clemens was a country boy who enjoyed hunting and all traditional country activities. He also grew up knowing that his family had provided prince-bishops for the Church over the generations. It came as no surprise when he went to study for the priesthood. But as a young priest he made great sacrifices—turning away from country pursuits which he loved, he devoted himself with vigour to the poor in the parish in Berlin where he was assigned. When the First World War brought hardship and hunger, he worked to distribute whatever relief was available. He remained a staunch monarchist and was wary of anything left-wing.

In 1933 Father von Galen was appointed Bishop of Munster. These were tumultuous years in Germany. The Nazis had come to power. Another war was looming. Bishop von Galen was a patriot. He loved his homeland and taught others to do so too. He had little time for the Nazis, and opposed them openly when they started to take over Church properties and forcing nuns and monks to leave.

The Nazis were beginning to arrest people and imprison them without trial. They taught that Christianity belonged to the past and that the future would have no place for such old-fashioned things. Bishop von Galen was one of a group of German bishops who were called to Rome by the Pope because he was so anxious about what was happening: when they gave him details of the grim situation prepared a special letter to the German people begging them to turn back from this path. It began "Mit brenneder sorge" — "with burning anxiety".

But the Nazis continued in power and in 1939 Germany invaded Poland and war broke out. Bishop von Galen loved Germany but he could not be silent in the face of injustice. People were being arrested because they opposed the Nazi government.

Speaking from the pulpit of his church in Munster, Bishop von Galen denounced what was happening: "None of us is safe—even some one who knows he is the most loyal and conscientious of citizens and conscious of his complete innocence cannot be sure that he will not some day be deported from his home, deprived of his freedom and locked up in the cellars and concentration camps of the Gestapo [the State Secret Police]". As Bishop, he called for justice. "Justice is the only solid foundation of any state. The right to life, to inviolability, to freedom is an indispensable part of any moral order of society ... We demand justice! If this call remains unheard and unanswered, if the rule of justice is not restored, then our German people and our country—in spite of the heroism of our soldiers and the glorious victories they have won—will perish through an inner rottenness and decay."

In 1941 people began to discover that something terrible was happening in German clinics and institutions for the mentally ill and the handicapped: people were being killed. Bishop von Galen wrote to the authorities to find out if the rumours were true. He received no reply. Evidence began to pile up—people were puzzled to discover the disappearance of their relatives and friends. What was happening to them? From the pulpit of his church, the Bishop asked the same questions. He described how his questions had been evaded again and again, and how he had discovered that there was indeed a programme of planned killing which was being steadily implemented:

> We must expect, therefore, that the poor defenceless patients are, sooner or later, going to be killed. Why?... because in the judgement of some official body, on the decision of some committee, they have become "unworthy to live", because they are classed as "unproductive members of the national community". The judgment is that they can no longer produce

any goods: they are like an old piece of machinery which no longer works, like an old horse
which has become incurably lame, like a cow
which no longer gives any milk. What happens
to an old piece of machinery? It is thrown on
the scrap heap. What happens to a lame horse,
an unproductive cow? I will not pursue the
comparison to the end—so fearful is its appro-
priateness and its illuminating power ... If it is
once admitted that men have the right to kill
"unproductive" fellowmen—even though it is
at present applied only to poor and defenceless
mentally ill patients—then the way is open for
the murder of all unproductive men and
women: the incurably ill, those disabled in
industry or war. The way is open, indeed, for
the murder of all of us, when we become old
and infirm and therefore unproductive.

People were appalled to learn of what was happening.
They had been told that Germany had gone to war to
defend itself, but this was not the case. What was going
on? The Bishop gave specific examples "I will give you
an example of what is happening. One of the patients
in Marienthal was a man of 55, a farmer from a country
parish in the Münster region—I could give you his
name—who has suffered for some years from mental
disturbance and was therefore admitted to Marienthal
hospital. He was not mentally ill in the full sense: he
could receive visits and was always happy when his
relatives came to see him. Only a fortnight ago he was
visited by his wife and one of his sons, a soldier on
home leave from the front. The son is much attached
to his father, and the parting was a sad one: no one
could tell whether the soldier would return and see
his father again, since he might fall in battle for his

country. The son, the soldier, will certainly never again see his father on earth, for he has since then been put on the list of the "unproductive". A relative, who wanted to visit the father this week in Marienthal, was turned away with the information that the patient had been transferred elsewhere on the instructions of the Council of State for National Defence. No information could be given about where he had been sent, but the relatives would be informed within a few days. What information will they be given? The same as in other cases of the kind? That the man has died, that his body has been cremated, that the ashes will be handed over on payment of a fee? Then the soldier, risking his life in the field for his fellow-countrymen, will not see his father again on earth, because fellow-countrymen at home have killed him."

The Bishop's sermons caused a stir, and copies of them began to circulate in Germany. The Allies who were fighting Germany regarded him as a hero, and reports of his sermons appeared in British newspapers. The Nazis, of course, were furious. Some of the Nazi leaders wanted to arrest him right away, but others knew that if they did that, all the people of Munster would rise up—they loved their bishop and they regarded him as their leader and their hero. What to do? So, instead, the Nazis started arresting the Bishop's priests and helpers—they were taken away to prisons and concentration camps while the Bishop—who by now had lost his home in a bombing raid and was living on the outskirts in a borrowed room—tried to find out what was happening.

The old laws of Germany were still in force: murder was a crime. The Bishop formally denounced the killers of the helpless and the handicapped as murderers, and called on the authorities to arrest them. But nothing was done. Instead Bishop von Galen's own life and freedom were at stake.

By now the war was reaching its height, and German cities were being bombed day and night with many people being killed. The cathedral in Munster was in ruins, families were living in the shells of their homes or in air-raid shelters, many people were missing, food and basic household goods were hard to find.

The fighting went on and the Allies invaded, finally reaching Germany and defeating the German armies. Now there could be peace—but the people were starving, desperate for news of their missing husbands and fathers and sons who had been fighting on various fronts, and confused about what would happen to them in the future. The Bishop spent the weeks and months after the war ended trying to help people. The Allies respected him because of his anti-Nazi views, and he alone could try to speak up for the defeated German people who were beginning to realise how wrong it had been to allow the Nazis to take power.

The Pope created Bishop von Galen a Cardinal and he was able, with great difficulty, to get to Rome to receive the honour. When he returned, everyone in the ruined city of Munster turned out to cheer him. But he was ill and exhausted. He died only a short while later. He did not live to see the cathedral rebuilt or a new non-Nazi Germany slowly emerge. But his name is today honoured in Munster—and by the Church which has now declared him Blessed Claus von Galen. Many people also still remember him by the name that he was given in the war years the "lion of Munster".

20

MARCEL CALLO—
PATRON OF YOUTH

LIFE SEEMED HAPPY and good for young Marcel Callo as he entered his twenties, even though the times were hard and his country, France, was caught up in the horror of the Second World War. Marcel came from a loving and affectionate family, and he was engaged to be married to a beautiful girl, and above all he had his Catholic Faith and was very active with the "Jocists", the Young Christian Workers. They met regularly to pray together, and to help spread the Gospel among their friends, using the motto "See, judge, act". When he had first started work at a print factory he had been hurt and horrified by the dirty crude sexual jokes of his fellow workers. But his quiet efforts to show a Christian spirit began to change things. The Young Christian Workers gained respect for their beliefs. They showed that the Christian faith really mattered. Some of the older people in the Church found them quite revolutionary: they found new ways to express their faith and they wanted to be missionaries to their own generation.

In 1943, tragedy struck the Callo family when Marcel's younger sister Marie-Madeline was killed in an air raid. Not long afterwards, Marcel received official call-up papers: he had to go to forced-labour in Germany. His fiancée came with him to the railway station. They had always prayed together, and had promised to dedicate their whole future to God. Now, as they said goodbye, she had a sudden very deep sense that this was not just a temporary farewell but something far more serious. They spoke together about trusting in God and she even mentioned martyrdom. But Marcel said he could surely never be a martyr because he was not worthy of that.

Conditions were difficult for the French labourers in Germany and at first he was very homesick. In particular, he missed his beloved fiancée. He tried very hard not to give in to feelings of loneliness and misery, but he was frequently unwell and, along with everyone else, suffered from the poor food and lack of everyday comforts.

He prayed, and, as he later wrote to his fiancée: "One day Christ answered me. He told me I was not to give in to despair; that I should take care of my fellow workers — and I found joy again." He was able to make contact with some fellow-Jocists. They started to pray together, and arranged for a priest to celebrate Mass. They encouraged one another and helped others to rediscover the joy and beauty of the Christian faith. Life for everyone began to have a new sense of meaning and purpose.

The Gestapo, the Nazi secret police, did not like this at all. The French were the enemy, and as labourers in Germany they might make trouble. One evening Marcel was suddenly arrested. No reason was given, but the Gestapo official simply told him that he was "too Catholic". He was interrogated, and then sent to a concentration camp, first at Flossenburg and then to Mauthausen in Austria.

He tried to remain cheerful and to help others. He was able to write letters home and in them he still expressed hope for the future.

But at Mauthausen the conditions were terrible. The men were forced to work for long hours in brutal conditions in a factory making aircraft parts. Guards beat them with rubber truncheons on the slightest excuse. Worst of all, someone stole Marcel's glasses— he was very shortsighted so this meant that in struggling to see enough to work and avoid more beatings, his eyes became sore and infected. He became weak and ill, and collapsed. There were no proper medical facilities. The sick were simply dumped in a filthy place with no treatments. On 19 March 1945, he died. Tragically, the war was in its very last days, and freedom for Marcel and for the other prisoners was near at hand.

Marcel's family only learned of his death some weeks later, in June. By then, the war had ended, and everyone was eagerly seeking news of released prisoners. But Marcel would never come home. A fellow prisoner from Mauthausen sought the family out and brought them the news of Marcel's death—in the last weeks of the war it had not been possible to send any letters.

Slowly, the Callo family began to hear from people who had lived and worked with Marcel, and learned how he had transformed the lives of his fellow workers during the terrible weeks in Mauthausen—how his faith had brought them meaning and hope, how they had come to understand that God was real and that even suffering was not completely pointless. Men spoke about how their lives had changed since meeting

Marcel and how they had become practising Catholics,
living the Faith and attending Mass regularly.

Marcel came to be an example of how faith and
courage can give life meaning even if terrible things
happen. Most significantly of all, Catholics in Austria
and Germany came to learn about him, and to be
touched and inspired by his story. He became a symbol
of reconciliation and peace. In 1987 he was beatified
by Pope John Paul II.

In 2002 Blessed Marcel Callo became a patron of
World Youth Day, in which young Catholics from
across the world come together to pray and celebrate
Mass. For all young people, especially those just
starting work, he is a patron saint, praying for them
from Heaven.

21

JOSEF SLIPYJ, WITNESS TO THE GULAG

N THE TWENTIETH century, there were more Christian martyrs than in all the other centuries put together. A great number of these were martyred under Communism, the terrible scourge which began in Russia in 1917. The Bolsheviks took control of Russia in a coup, and were able to do so as a result of the tragic circumstances of the First World War. In the 1920s and 30s—and then on through the 1940s and 50s and right through until the final collapse of Communism in 1990, Russia and its satellite countries tried to enforce atheism. The official Marxist-Leninist teaching was that God did not exist, and that churches existed only to prolong old-fashioned ideas which were opposed to the Communist Revolution and which must therefore be crushed. People could be arrested simply for living in a village and having a fondness for the local church and for old customs.

Thus, from 1917 onwards, Christians were persecuted, churches closed, children drilled in atheism in schools and youth groups. Christians were not the only ones singled out: to belong to any group that seemed to "oppose the Revolution" could mean arrest. Under the evil dictator Stalin in the 1930s, in what became known as the Great Terror, the police were simply given quotas of people to arrest—they had to round up a certain number of people each day and they would do so by seizing people at random, from their homes at night or from their workplaces during the day, and taking them off to prison and from there to forced-labour in remote camps, from which most never returned. To this day, there are families who simply do not know what became of some of their relatives during those years.

We do not know the names of all the countless people who died in the dreadful labour-camps in the bitter cold beyond the Arctic Circle, in filth and hunger, far from their homes and families, frightened and believing themselves forgotten. And in Ukraine, which was annexed by the Soviet Union, millions of people died of starvation, as all the crops were systematically taken by Government forces: people were reduced to eating grass, the straw from the thatch of their houses, and even the bodies of people who had already died.

Cardinal Josef Slipyj, a Bishop of the Ukrainian Catholic church, was imprisoned for many years in a labour-camp. His story serves as a witness to all the misery that was brought about by Communism. In telling his story, we connect with all the millions whose stories are unknown.

He was born in 1892 and studied for the priesthood in the Greek-Catholic Rite first at Lviv in Ukraine and then at Innsbruck in Austria, and was ordained in 1917. As a young priest, he went to Rome for further studies, and was there until 1922 when he returned to his home country and taught at the seminary in Lviv. He eventually became the Rector there. Lviv was at that time part of Poland. But in 1939 the Second World War broke out, and Germany invaded Poland from the

West, Russia from the East. Lviv was in the Eastern part and the future for Father Josef Slipyj was now to be bound up with the Soviet Empire.

In December 1939 he was ordained as Archbishop of Lviv. It was clear to everyone in the Church that grim times lay ahead. His ordination was carried out in secrecy—already the Soviet authorities were taking far too much interest in the activities of the Greek Catholic Church.

In November 1944 Metropolitan Andrej Sheptytsky, the head of the Greek Catholic Church died and Archbishop Slipyj took his place. Only a short while later he was arrested. He had made clear his dislike of the Soviet regime, and this was announced as meaning that he fully supported the German invasion of Ukraine. He was sentenced to eight years in prison-camps, but would actually serve for longer. Meanwhile the Greek Catholic Church was forcibly "merged" with the Orthodox Church, which meant that it no longer officially existed. Greek-Catholics had to worship secretly, out in the forests or in people's homes, or wherever they could gather without danger of arrest.

There were international protests against Archbishop Slipyj's imprisonment and finally, as a result of protests from the American President John F. Kennedy, and from the Pope, he was set free. He was even able to go to Rome to take part in the great Vatican Council that took place in 1965. By that time he had spent nearly twenty years in prison and in labour-camps.

He would later recall "I had to suffer imprisonment by night, secret court-rooms, endless interrogations and spying upon me, moral and physical maltreatment and humiliation, torture, and enforced starvation. In front of the evil interrogators and judged I stood, a helpless prisoner and silent witness of the Church who, physically and psychologically exhausted, was giving testimony to his native Church, itself silent and doomed to die.

> As a prisoner for the sake of Christ I found strength throughout my own Way of the Cross in the realization that my spiritual flock, my own native Ukrainian people, all the bishops, priests and faithful—fathers and mothers, children, and dedicated youth as well as the helpless old people, were walking beside me along the same path. I was not alone!

Those who were with him in prison-camps remember him being beaten and unable to walk properly. In the bitter cold he suffered from frostbite. Along with the other prisoners he suffered from the bugs that infested the cells, so that they were bitten as they tried to sleep. It was impossible to wash properly—all the prisoners were itching with lice.

When Cardinal Slipyj—he had been made a Cardinal secretly and in his absence by Pope Pius XII in the 1950s—arrived in Rome in 1963 he was limping and weak. He was taken to a monastery and later remembered the drink of hot milk that he was given. A new life opened for him—that of an exile, and a spokesman for his martyred Church.

Cardinal Slipyj was not always an easy man with whom to work over the next years. He sought to defend all the rights and traditions of his Church. He would not waver or negotiate if he thought that the traditions of his Greek Catholic heritage were at stake. But he was honoured because of the suffering that he endured, and because of his strong faith and his loyalty, which had never wavered. When he died in 1984, people spoke of him as a saint and today the process for his possible Beatification has been begun.

Under Pope John Paul II, and with the collapse of Communism, the Greek Catholic Church flourished again. Today, Ukraine is free from the terror of the Communist days. A statue of Cardinal Slipyj stands in Ternopil, his birthplace, and his body is in an honoured grave in the cathedral at Lviv. Future generations will be told about his life, and about the courage and faith that was needed to endure in the time of persecution.

22

FATHER JERZY, HERO OF POLAND

OU PRONOUNCE HIS name Yer-jee. It's the Polish way of saying "George". Polish names seem odd to us, and Father Jerzy's surname is quite hard to pronounce: Popiełuszko—pop-ee-woosh-ko. His story is a very important one: he was a great hero with a message for today. He was born in 1947, a couple of years after the Second World War. It was a tragic and difficult time for Poland. The Soviet Union, with its Communist government, had taken charge of Poland, its Red Army marching in as the war ended. Millions of Polish people had been killed in the war, and those who were left were poor, their capital city Warsaw was in ruins, there was little food, everything was in confusion as men were missing or wounded or in prison camps.

But the Polish people were Catholics. They held fast to their faith even though the Communists did not want them to do so. As Jerzy grew up, he knew that being true to the Church, being faithful to God, was the central reality in life. He knew that he wanted to be a priest.

Jerzy was ordained in 1972. The Communists forced all young men, including those who wanted to be priests, to serve in the Army. While Jerzy was doing his military service, he was bullied and treated badly as the authorities wanted to make him lose his Christian faith and abandon all ideas of the priesthood. But he was able to hold his own in arguments and once his military service was completed he began training for the priesthood at the seminary.

As a young priest, he went to work in a busy parish. He was popular with children and young people: he loved to teach, to help young people to pray and to have a real encounter with Christ as redeemer and Saviour at the heart of their lives.

Following a bad illness at the end of his military service, Father Jerzy never had good health. But this did not stop him working hard. He was given special responsibility for medical students and for nurses. He gathered them together to pray and study together about the great issues of their lives: the importance of God and of giving the best possible care to the sick, the idea of neighbourliness and service. This did not make him popular with the Communist authorities. They wanted all Poland's young people simply to be taught that there is no God, and that the Communist state solves all their problems. They did not like the idea of a young and dedicated priest inspiring young people with a larger and nobler message.

In 1978 Pope John Paul II was elected—a Pope from Poland. In 1979 be returned to Poland on a triumphal pilgrimage. Everyone knew that nothing would now stay the same. The following year workers united to form Solidarity—a genuine and free trade union, fighting for people's rights and for a better way ahead.

By now Fr Jerzy was in charge of a big church in Warsaw, St Stanislaus Koska. When the men of Solidarity staged a strike at the local steelworks, they asked for a priest to come and say Mass for them.

Cardinal Wyszinski, the Archbishop of Warsaw, agreed, but the priest he wanted to send was unable to do so. Father Jerzy went in his place. He was about to take part in something extraordinary—a strike, organised by men who wanted real freedom and a decent life for their families, in a country dominated by a cruel and oppressive government which had brought misery and poverty to the nation. And these strikers were Catholic: for them, having Mass was central to life. Their faith was at the heart of their campaign.

Father Jerzy would later remember that walk to the steelworks:

> I will never forget that day and that Mass. As I was making my way to the steelworks, I felt a great stage fear. This was a totally new experi-ence. I kept asking myself many questions. What will I find? How will they welcome me? Will there be enough room for saying Mass? Who will do the Scripture readings and the singing? These may seem very naive questions today, but at that time they were like arrows darting at me … When I approached the gate of the steel-works I had the first surprise. I saw a thick row of people who were smiling and crying simultaneously. When they applauded, I thought someone important was following me. I soon found out the applause was for me, the first priest ever to pass through the gate of the steelworks. At that point I realised this cheerful welcome was actually addressed to the Church, which had been patiently knocking at the gates of Polish factories for thirty long years. My misgivings were needless, as everything had been made ready for Mass. In the middle of the factory square there was an altar with a

cross and even a makeshift confessional. The
said cross was later dug in near the gate of the
steelworks. It has survived hard times and has
stood unshaken till now, always decorated with
fresh flowers. Readers volunteered. You should
hear the voices of those men who had often
used a coarse language and were now reading
the Holy Scriptures with piety. Later on thousands of people proclaimed "Thanks be to
God!" It turned out that even the singing was
much better than it often is inside churches.

That big steelworkers strike was followed by other
dramatic events Nothing would ever be the same in
Poland again. When the Government reacted with
force and eventually declared military law across the
country, Father Jerzy—by now a well-known figure
associated with Solidarity—began celebrating a special
"Mass for the Fatherland" each week, a Mass for
Poland, praying for the nation and its future. Hundreds, and then thousands, of young people came.
Father Jerzy spoke about the need to speak the truth,
about courage, about God's loving care of each indi-
vidual and each family. Communism had signally
failed to answer everyday human needs—and had no
answer whatever for the deep questions raised about
life itself, about suffering and injustice and about
people's hopes and the longing for the good and the
true and the beautiful.

Many people were angry: the Communists had been
in power for years and years and had always told lies,
conditions in factories were grim, everyone knew that
over the years the police had been involved with brutal
beatings and torture. It would have been easy to
inflame people into angry mobs who would have tried
to create a rebellion, which would have been hopeless

as the Government had the Army, tanks, and guns—
there would have been a massacre. There must be
peaceful change. The message of truth and hope would
prevail. "Overcome evil with good" was the strong,
consistent message that Father Jerzy preached and
lived, day after day.

Fr Jerzy was being immensely brave in doing this.
It was dangerous to speak out. Police spies came and
listened to his sermons. He was arrested and interrogated again and again. His home was burgled in
mysterious circumstances. He was involved in two
major car crashes that seemed to have been pre-ar-
ranged.. The young people who came to his Masses
tried to protect him: they begged him not to go out
alone, they accompanied him on visits and errands,
and urged him not to answer the door to strangers.

It could not last. Within the secret police, decisions
were made. Young Father Jerzy had to be eliminated.
Some one had to deal with him. It was all possible in
a Communist state: plenty of people opposed to the
regime had been killed over the years. For the first
decades of Communism in Poland it was easy to
arrange: the police arrived at some one's home in the
middle of the night, entered by force and hurled him
into a police van. He would end up in a labour-camp
somewhere in Siberia, dying eventually amid the bitter
cold and the filth and hunger. His family would plead
in vain for information. Anyone who asked too often
or too publicly would be killed or would mysteriously
disappear. Everyone would be frightened. Questions
would remain unanswered.

But now that Solidarity had been started, nothing
was so simple. They would have to do things secretly.
In October 1984 men from the secret police, posing as

traffic policemen, stopped Fr Jerzy's car and kid-
napped him. They beat him savagely, tied him up and
threw him into the boot of their car. When he managed
to struggle free they beat him again and gagged him,
tying a weight round his feet and making a noose so
that as he struggled he choked. We do not know
whether he died in the car or whether or not he
drowned when they threw him, still tied up and with
weights attached, into a river.

His body was not found for several days. The young
people at his church gathered as soon as they realised
he was missing. Day after day they prayed. The
crowds built up. The disappearance of Fr Jerzy could
not be kept secret. Foreign television and newspapers
started to take an interest. Eventually the outcry could
not be contained: "Where is Fr Jerzy?" His body was
found. There was terrible evidence of the brutality with
which he had been treated. All of Poland was plunged
into mourning. Various official versions of his death
were announced but were not believed. His funeral
became a national event. His grave became a place
where pilgrim gathered to pray. They took as their
theme the message that he had consistently taught in
his sermons: "Overcome evil with good". When they
prayed the Our Father, they said three times "forgive
us our trespasses, as we forgive those who trespass
against us". They would not allow their grief to turn
into hatred or revenge. They stayed faithful to Fr
Jerzy's message.

Full freedom came to Poland in 1989. Solidarity
signed an agreement that ensured that Communism
no longer dominated the country. Then finally free
elections were held. A whole new chapter of history

had opened up: Poland could be a free and prosperous and normal country.

In 2010 the Church officially declared Father Jerzy to be a martyr: he is now Blessed Jerzy Popieluszko. He is a great hero in Poland and thousands and thousands of people visit his grave at the church where he worked, St Stanislaus Koska in Warsaw. All around his grave are stones arranged to form a giant rosary, making a shape of the map of Poland. The cross of the rosary marks his actual tomb. Blessed Jerzy is a patron saint of young people, of all men who work in factories in harsh conditions, and of all people who struggle for freedom and for basic human rights. His feast-day is 19 October.

23

CHRISTIAN DE CHERGÉ AND THE ATLAS MONKS

HRISTIAN DE CHERGÉ was born into a French aristocratic family, one of seven children. His father was serving as a soldier and when Christian was small the family lived in Algeria. Here, he saw Moslems at prayer and his mother told him "Remember, they pray to the same God as we do".

When he grew up, Christian himself served in the Army and volunteered to go to Algeria, at that time still ruled by France but about to become independent. Here, he renewed his love for the land and his interest in Islam. On one occasion, a Moslem friend, Mohammed, saved his life—as they walked along together, an attacker pounced, and Mohammed leapt to protect his friend, standing between him and the weapon. Some days later, Mohammed was found dead. Christian never forgot this.

At the age of twenty, Christian entered religious life. He was ordained as a priest and served for a while in Paris, including work as a school chaplain. But he sensed that his real calling was to monastic life in an Islamic country. He studied Arabic in Rome, and went to stay every year at a Benedictine abbey in Morocco. Finally he was settled at the monastery of Tibhirine in

Algeria, where in due course he was elected Abbot of the small community of nine monks.

The monks were Trappists. They lived a regulated life of prayer and work, with much silence. They had a great bond with the local people, and there were Christian/Islamic dialogues in Tibhirine, both formal and informal. The aim was not only friendship but something more—a genuine search for spiritual truths, for a sense of union with God and a rich understanding of the importance of prayer. Father Christian spoke about what Christians could learn from the idea of submission to God as understood by devout Moslems.

Sadly, extremist groups within the Algerian community were stirring up anti-Christian and anti-French feeling. The monks knew that their lives were under threat. It was suggested that they take the prudent way, and leave. Abbot Christian asked all in the community to pray about this, and then, without any hurry, a vote was taken. It was decided that they would stay. They were on good terms with the local people, even those who had close links to terrorist groups. They knew and loved the genuine religious faith of so many of the ordinary peaceful followers of Islam.

But the politics of the day were against them. The terrorist groups were small but passionate and effective, especially among the young. In May 1996 kidnappers forced their way into the monastery and took away seven of the monks, among them Father Christian. Two other monks were in other rooms and were not found by the kidnappers. They tried to raise the alarm but found that the telephone wires had been cut. It was only the next morning that they were able to get to the nearest town and try to summon help. The seven missing monks were not found for many weeks, and then their bodies were discovered. They had been beheaded. The exact circumstances of their deaths are not known.

Father Christian, knowing what the future might hold, had written a letter to be opened after his death.

> If it should happen one day—and it could be today—that I become a victim of the terrorism which now seems ready to encompass all the foreigners in Algeria, I would like my community, my Church, my family, to remember that my life was *given* to God and to this country. To accept that the One Master of all life was not a stranger to this brutal departure. I would like them to pray for me: how worthy would I be found of such an offering?

> I would like them to be able to associate this death with so many other equally violent ones allowed to fall into the indifference of anonymity. My life has no more value than any other. Nor any less value. In any case, it has not the innocence of childhood. I have lived long enough to know that I share in the evil which seems, alas, to prevail in the world, and even in that which would strike me blindly. I should like, when the time comes, to have a space of lucidity which would enable me to beg forgiveness of God and of my fellow human beings, and at the same time to forgive with all my heart the one who would strike me down.

> I could not desire such a death. It seems to me important to state this. I don't see, in fact, how I could rejoice if the people I love were indiscriminately accused of my murder. It would be too high a price to pay for what will be called,

perhaps, the "grace of martyrdom" to owe this to an Algerian, whoever he may be, especially if he says he is acting in fidelity to what he believes to be Islam.

I know the contempt in which Algerians taken as a whole can be engulfed. I know, too, the caricatures of Islam which encourage a certain idealism. It is too easy to give oneself a good conscience in identifying this religious way with the fundamentalist ideology of its extremists. For me, Algeria and Islam is something different. It is a body and a soul. I have proclaimed it often enough, I think, in view of and in the knowledge of what I have received from it, finding there so often that true strand of the Gospel learned at my mother's knee, my very first Church, precisely in Algeria, and already respecting believing Muslims.

My death, obviously, will appear to confirm those who hastily judged me naive or idealistic: "Let him tell us now what he thinks of it!" But these must know that my insistent curiosity will then be set free. This is what I shall be able to do, if God wills: Immerse my gaze in that of the Father, to contemplate with Him His children of Islam as He sees them, all shining with the glory of Christ, fruit of His Passion, filled with the Gift of the Spirit whose secret joy will always be to establish communion and to refashion the likeness, playing with the differences.

This life lost, totally mine and totally theirs, I thank God who seems to have wished it entirely for the sake of that JOY in and in spite of everything. In this THANK YOU which is said for everything in my life, from now on, I certainly include you, friends of yesterday and today, and you, O my friends of this place, besides my mother and father, my sisters and brothers and their families, a hundredfold as was promised!

And you too, my last minute friend, who will not know what you are doing, Yes, for you too I say this THANK YOU AND THIS "A-DIEU" — to commend you to this God in whose face I see yours. And may we find each other, happy "good thieves" in Paradise, if it pleases God, the Father of us both ... AMEN!

24

FATHER PINO, MARTYRED BY THE MAFIA

ATHER GIUSEPPE "PINO" Puglisi was appointed parish priest of a small village called Godrana in the South of Italy, in the 1960s. There were only about a hundred people living in the village, but it had a very high murder rate. Thanks to a passionate rivalry between two gangs, there had been fifteen murders in the village in the few years just before his arrival.

Father Pino prayed and started to go from house to house in the village, reading the Gospel with the families. His theme was forgiveness. He formed neighbourhood groups in which people would get together—initially once a month, but then, as it all became popular, fortnightly. And things in the village began to change. A woman whose son had been murdered told the priest that she knew she must forgive the mother of the murderer. After a great deal of prayer, and negotiation by the priest, the two women met. They spoke together and prayed together. They eventually were able to establish a bond of friendship. Bit by bit, the whole atmosphere in the village began to change. The longstanding hatreds and rivalries slowly crumbled.

Fr Pino used to say 'Peace is like bread—it has to be shared in order to be savoured.'

He had always wanted to be a priest, and went to the seminary to train when he was sixteen years old. After some years in the village of Godrana he was sent to a much bigger parish, a town with some 8,000 people, San Gaetano. Here, everything seemed to be hopeless and run-down. The old church was extremely small—only just over 100 people could be fitted in at any one time—and was in poor repair with a leaking roof. There was much corruption among the local officials, and a huge and sinister Mafia presence. Organised crime seemed to be everywhere. Young people were offered cheap goods—motorbikes, even cars—that they knew to be stolen. Anyone who tried to organise some local community initiative—caring for the needy or raising funds for charity—could expect to get their home vandalised and their children threatened.

Father Pino openly opposed the Mafia, and showed people that they must conquer fear with courage and love. For years, Mafia bosses gave money to the church and insisted that their "men of honour" headed up parish processions: Father Pino refused the money and banned the men from leading the processions. He taught the children not to accept stolen goods. He refused to join in the general acceptance of the paying of bribes for necessary local improvements in basic things like sewage and road works. He spoke openly about the ridiculous situation which had emerged in which ordinary civic life depended on corruption, with everyone knowing that bribes were offered and taken, and brutal thuggery used as a method of controlling anyone who opposed the Mafia gangs.

People began to discover that they could trust Father Pino. In addition to his work in the parish, he taught in a local high school. He had a good influence on the local young people. They began to feel confident about rejecting offers from the Mafia, and to form instead normal friendships among themselves based on trust. The public services were affected too: it wasn't normal to have to bribe people any more. It became possible to get sewage problems fixed and roadworks done.

But there was a price to be paid. Fr Pino knew what had happened to others who had opposed the Mafia. Homes had been burned and people had been beaten, with death threats made.

The parish was a busy one, with plenty for the priest to do. On his 56th birthday in September 1993, Father Pino officiated at two weddings, and also met some parents to plan baptism arrangements for their children. Then there was a little party with friends to celebrate his birthday. Finally, he drove home. It was a little before half past eight in the evening.

Two men stopped him as he got out of his car. One whipped out a gun which had a silencer on it, held it to Fr Pino's head and shot him at point-blank range.

Fr Pino's murder shocked the town. Huge crowds attended his funeral. There was an outcry against the Mafia. Fr Pino was hailed as a martyr. When the two murderers were arrested, one of them admitted his guilt and described Father Pino's last moments. The priest, he said, knew what was going to happen and told the men 'I've been expecting you'.

Father Pino's courage had changed people's ideas about themselves. He had known the risks he was taking. But he had gone ahead and resisted evil, and taught firmly about not giving in to bullying, and not accepting theft and bribery. He had given ordinary families a sense of their own dignity and worth. The evil grip of the Mafia could be broken—but it needed courage to speak the truth, and to live the truth, day after day.

In 2012 Father Pino was officially declared to be a Martyr, honoured by the Catholic Church, and he was beatified on 26 May 2013.

25

THE GREAT JOHN PAUL

I N 1920 A baby boy was born to a family in
Poland. They named him Karol—the Polish
version of Charles. He would grow up to be
one of the most famous men in the world. Young Karol
was a bright and gifted boy—good at sports and at
lessons. His childhood was marked by sadness—his
mother died when he was only six and just a few years
later his beloved older brother, Edmund, also died.
Karol and his father were left alone together.

In 1939 Germany invaded Poland, and five terrible
years of war were to follow. Karol had enrolled as a
student at the Jagiellonian University in Krakow but
that was now closed and all of the professors were sent
to concentration camps. Karol had to go to work in a
stone quarry—long hours in tough conditions. During
this time, his father, who was by now elderly, died. At
twenty years of age, Karol had lost his entire immediate family.

When the war ended, freedom did not come to
Poland. The country was taken over by the Red Army
and a Communist government was imposed. By now
Karol had made the biggest and most important
decision of his life—to become a priest. During the
war, this meant studying secretly because the Germans
had closed all the colleges. Under the Communists,
being a priest would be hard and challenging, because

they believed that the Church should die, and they did not allow Catholics any real freedom.

Young Father Karol became a much-loved, hard-working and popular priest. He took groups of young people out into the mountains, hiking and canoeing. Here they could be free. They could pray together, and talk about God, about the big issues in life, about love and friendship and their hopes for the future.

The Communists spied on all priests. When Father Karol was appointed a Bishop, and later an Archbishop they tried to make life difficult for him. But he was always open and unafraid. When the Communist authorities refused to allow permission for a church to be built, Archbishop Karol went to celebrate Mass with the local people in the open air again and again. Finally, they won the right to build the church and Archbishop Karol was able to consecrate it. The Catholic people of Krakow loved him—he was their leader, a man they could trust. He lived a simple lifestyle, even when he was appointed a Cardinal, giving away his good clothes and books to the poor and making do with things that were old and worn. He still went hiking with groups in the mountains. He was a popular teacher, young people packing out his lectures at the university. He loved to gather people together to sing old songs. And he showed them all how to pray—he spent a long time in prayer each day.

In 1978 Pope Paul VI died, and all the Cardinals went to Rome to elect a new Pope. They chose Cardinal Albino Luciani, from Venice, a good and popular man. He took the name John Paul I. But no one knew that in fact he was ill—and sadly he died just a month after being elected. The Cardinals met again. This time they elected Cardinal Karol Woytila. It was staggering—a

great moment of history. There had never before been
a Polish Pope! For centuries, all the Popes had been
Italian. And this new Pope was extraordinary! When
he appeared on the balcony at St Peter's in Rome, he
greeted everyone in a friendly way and even joked
with them. Everyone sensed that a new era was beginning.

As Pope, Cardinal Woytila took the name John Paul
II. From the start, he made it clear that he wanted to
take the message of Jesus Christ to every part of the
world. He told everyone "Do not be afraid!" He
emphasised that everything should be open to Christ—
this spelt true freedom.

Pope John Paul's first big international visit was to
Mexico. The government there had placed many
restrictions on the Church, and Catholics had suffered
much over the years. Many were also poor, and
struggling to find jobs to support their families. John
Paul's visit brought them together in hope and joy. It
gave them new confidence. The old restrictions melted
away and the Church gathered strength.

The Communist authorities in Poland were afraid.
They tried very hard to stop John Paul from visiting
Poland. But in the end they had to allow it. And the
Polish people in their millions turned out to greet him.
They lined the streets, they threw flowers in his path,
they waved flags and decorated their houses with
welcoming banners—and they poured into the great
square in the centre of Warsaw, the capital, where he
was to celebrate Mass. No one who was there—or who
watched it on television—would ever forget this Mass.
Pope John Paul's strong clear voice spoke of eternal
truths. He spoke about the Holy Spirit and called on

Him to descend on the land and renew it. He spoke with confidence about God, and about human dignity.

For long, long years the Polish people had had to endure enforced restrictions on their freedom. Life was harsh, with long working hours and poor pay. It was hard to obtain basic things: shoes, soap, decent clothes. Those in authority had access to special shops from which ordinary people were banned. Communism was unjust—and it didn't allow any opposition. The Catholic faith could not be taught in schools. Catholic books and newspapers were restricted.

Now the Pope had come to Poland—a Polish people, who knew and understood all that they had endured and suffered together for so long. He spoke from the heart, and they knew it. Nothing would ever be the same again. The Church in Poland erupted in joy. Young people saw the Pope as their hero.

But Pope John Paul's concern was not just with Poland. He travelled to other places, and he spoke to huge crowds in St Peter's Square in Rome: his message of hope and goodwill lifted people's hearts.

Those who hated the Church saw a danger. They hired a gunman, and on 13 May 1981 he shot the Pope at point-blank range in St Peter's Square. The Pope fell—the gunman had aimed straight and it seemed impossible that John Paul could survive. He was rushed to hospital. Everyone prayed and prayed. By a miracle, the Pope survived—the bullet had missed his vital organs by a tiny fraction of an inch, as if a gentle hand had reached from Heaven to save the Pope's life. He was in great pain but he recovered, and publicly forgave the man who had tried to murder him. The following year someone else tried to kill him—a priest from a breakaway group who wanted to get rid of him. He tried to stab the Pope and he drew blood, but was dragged away.

John Paul became perhaps the greatest missionary the Church has had since St Paul. He went to Africa, to America, to Asia. He communicated the joy and hope of the Catholic Faith in dozens of different languages, across the globe. He launched World Youth Day—young people coming together in vast numbers to celebrate their faith and pray together, building up a culture of peace for the future. He arranged for the publishing of a great new Catechism of the Catholic Church, so that people could learn and understood the beauty of the Catholic Faith. He called together representatives of all the world's main religions at Assisi to pray for peace.

Pope John Paul built a whole new friendship with the Jewish people. There had been many centuries of difficulties and injustice but now it was time for a fresh start. For the first time in nearly 2,000 years a Pope went to a synagogue: it was a beautiful moment, and it was just the beginning of a wonderful new time of goodwill and warmth between Christians and Jews.

As the year 2000 approached, Pope John Paul called the whole Church to renewal. He held a special service of repentance, saying "Sorry" for all the mistakes and injustices that the Church had carried out in the past. This opened the way to start the 21st century with clean hearts and a spirit of humility and hope.

Pope John Paul showed the world that to be Pope was not just to be a leader of Catholics, but a sign of God's love for everyone. The Christian church had long been divided—he brought Catholics and Protestants and Orthodox Christians together, inviting Prot-

estants and Orthodox preachers to preach in St Peter's
in Rome.

In Poland, everything changed: with their new-
found confidence, the Polish people found a united
voice. They launched a new movement, "Solidarity",
and eventually Communism was toppled. No one had
thought this would be possible. The Communists had
all the power—including the massive Red Army,
waiting in Russia to invade Poland if Communism was
threatened. But instead Communism was defeated,
and Poland gained freedom—and soon the Communists in Russia and elsewhere were toppled too.

John Paul always looked strong but in fact his health
was not good and he suffered a good deal. A tumour
had to be removed from his stomach, he broke a leg in
a fall, he had a big problem with a hip joint. Finally,
he contracted a disease which would cause him long,
slow suffering—Parkinson's Disease, which gradually
made it impossible for him to move or even to speak
easily. As he grew older, he could not walk anymore
and had to be wheeled in a chair. But he never gave
up work: he still taught and wrote and preached.
Young people loved him. People across the world
studied his teachings. Above all, he prayed, and he
taught people to pray. He had always loved the
Rosary, and as Pope he added five new "Mysteries"
to it—there had always been the Joyful, Sorrowful and
Glorious Mysteries and now he added the Luminous
Mysteries, the Mysteries of Light. The Rosary, which
had seemed old-fashioned, was taught to a new
generation and received a new importance.

When John Paul II died in 2005, the world grieved.
Thousands—and then it became millions—of people
flocked to Rome to pray at his funeral. They waited for

hours and hours to pass by his coffin. They prayed and sang. They wanted to thank him for giving the world a strong message of hope and for teaching everyone about God's love.

People spoke if him as a saint and at his funeral they held up banners saying "Santo subito" meaning "Make him a saint now!" And just six years after his death, the new Pope, Benedict XVI, was able to announce that John Paul was now officially Blessed John Paul, a first step on the way to sainthood. There has never been a Pope like Blessed John Paul, and many people call him John Paul the Great.

Lightning Source UK Ltd.
Milton Keynes UK
UKOW05f0056190713

214020UK00002B/12/P